George Washington Was a Badass:

Crazy But True Stories About
The United States' First President

BILL O'NEILL

ISBN: 978-1-64845-076-1

DON'T FORGET YOUR FREE BOOKS

GET THEM FOR FREE ON

WWW.TRIVIABILL.COM

TABLE OF CONTENTS

INTRODUCTION

It probably wouldn't be an overstatement to say that just about every adult *in the world* knows something about George Washington and that every American knows - or should know - a few more facts about the United States' first president. You probably know that, in addition to being the first American president, Washington was also his nation's first general and that he played a key role in the events leading up to the American Revolution.

But after that, what do you *really* know about George Washington?

In *George Washington Was a Badass: Some Truly Amazing Stories about the United States' First President*, we peel back the academic *and* popular veneer that normally covers books, articles, and documentaries about Washington and present you with a fresh new take on the Father of the Country. Like many other histories, this book follows Washington's career chronologically but instead of focusing on dates and places, it pays special attention to what made George Washington the USA's first true badass.

So, you're guaranteed to learn a lot about George Washington - probably a lot more than you already knew about him - *and* you'll have fun in the process. This is a history book, but it goes so far beyond a normal, boring one by lifting off the powdered wig of America's first president to see what kind of man rode on that fabled white horse.

You'll go on a journey to see what made Washington tick, why he was so important, and of course, what made him an epic badass!

We begin with how Washington began his life as a privileged yet truly American original, who always had an independent spirit and was a bit of a rebel inside. Unlike those of his same social class who grew up in England at the time, Washington was brought up in the fairly wild country of early 1700s Virginia, where even wealthy men had to learn how to shoot guns, chop wood, and live off the land.

Washington may have been born with wealth and status, but even in his childhood, he was often more comfortable around farmers, merchants, and sailors than he was in the upper class of society.

In other words, Washington's badass trajectory began early in his life.

And after childhood, Washington grew into being a badass young man who experienced the ups and downs of war and business at an age before most people today graduate from college.

Washington was so much of a badass that he didn't need to go to college anyway!

Then there was the American Revolution.

Of course, Washington became world-famous for leading the Continental Army to success against the British, and although he proved himself as a badass in numerous battles, he perhaps earned most of these badass bona fides off the battlefield. The Revolution was tough, to say the least, and it was especially so for Washington and his family. He sacrificed a lot to lead the troops and faced execution if defeated. Washington also suffered numerous setbacks on the battlefield that led many to question his leadership, but in the end, he was able to rise above all the doubts.

And that is probably most of all what made Washington such a badass.

George Washington had a seemingly uncanny ability to turn what appeared to be certain defeat or setbacks into victories. Maybe Washington was lucky, or maybe he had some kind of sixth sense that told him when to make a move and when not to, or maybe it was a combination of both. Whatever the case, whenever Washington was "down," he never sank too far, or stayed there too long.

He always got up, dusted the dirt off his blue coat, and went back onto the battlefield.

And time and time again, he was able to rally his men after losses to fight even harder and just as important, he became a symbol of hope for the new nation.

After winning the war, it was seen as academic that Washington would be the first leader of the new nation, but there were still plenty of challenges for him to face and opportunities for him to prove that he was still a badass, despite being up there in years.

George Washington was so badass that he was mythologized after he died. Although Washington certainly deserves all the praise historians give him today, he has become almost deified, and universally portrayed in a positive light. Even in the hyper-politicized world of today, where statues and monuments of many early American leaders are being torn down, Washington has escaped most major criticism and efforts to erase his name.

The fact that George Washington's legacy has for the most part transcended this harsh partisan political era is pretty badass in itself, don't you agree?

Keep reading to learn about just how much of a badass George Washington was in 30 short stories that follow his life and times. At the end of every chapter are a set of famous and memorable quotes said by Washington and others who knew him that relate to the themes of the specific chapters.

Open the book, turn the pages, and learn how, underneath his powdered wig, George Washington truly was America's first badass.

CHAPTER 1

A TRUE AMERICAN BADASS

At first glance, it may seem like George Washington had an easy, privileged life. After all, he did come from a fairly wealthy family that was also politically influential in the British colony of Virginia, but you have to consider the time and place where Washington was raised.

Even rich people had to be tough to be successful in the 1700s in Virginia.

It's true that George's ancestors were wealthy British plantation owners and that his father Augustine, who had added considerably to the family fortune, married a woman, Mary, from an equally wealthy and influential Virginia planter family. However, George didn't have all the benefits he would have had if he had grown up in England. And George didn't quite receive all the benefits his older brothers had received.

Well, I guess that depends on your perspective and how your upbringing molds you into the person you become in adulthood. The fact that George was never educated in England was seen by many in the 1700s polite American society as a curse, but it later turned out to be a blessing and one of the primary factors that made Washington a true badass.

The Wilds of Virginia

George Washington was born on February 22, 1732 in Popes Creek, Virginia. Although George was the oldest of Augustine and Mary's six children, Augustine was previously married and had two sons, Lawrence and Augustine Junior, who made it to adulthood. That fact alone should tell you that although the Washington's may have had money and influence, life in 1700s America could be quite precarious, even for the wealthy.

George's first lesson on the unpredictability of life in the wilds of Virginia came when Augustine died suddenly at the age of 49 when George was just 11.

It was definitely quite an emotional blow to the young boy, but young Washington quickly learned that there wasn't crying in 1700s Virginia. He had to pick himself and move on, as the oldest son of his parents.

From that point forward, George Washington had to grow up fast, with the role of father figure being filled by his older half-brother Lawrence.

Lawrence and Augustine Junior were formally educated in England, but George received his education in Virginia from tutors. The experience was one that shaped George's life in many ways, including how George saw himself and the world. George was bright and mechanically inclined, but he often found himself in conflict with others who had formal educations.

George Washington felt like he had something to prove around educated people and he sometimes despised those of his own class who would rather spend their time indoors.

George Washington, conversely, was a true, rugged outdoorsman, who had no problem doing manual labor, hunting, fishing, or cleaning the meat he took home. Washington may have been a wealthy and privileged individual, but he was a true American frontiersman. He saw the wilds of the New World yet to be tamed, but at the same time, he felt at home and akin to this wild new world.

Despite his wealth and influence, Washington was more comfortable talking to and being around American farmers, workers, and sailors than he was the British of his class. George Washington was a new kind of man in a new kind of world, which would help him become successful repeatedly throughout his life.

Quotes about Education and Knowledge

- "The best means of forming a manly, virtuous and happy people, will be found in the right education of youth. Without *this* foundation, every other means, in my opinion, must fail." - Washington in a letter to George Chapman on December 15, 1784.

- "A primary object should be the education of our youth in the science of government. In a republic, what species of knowledge can be equally important? And what duty more pressing than communicating it to those who are to be the future guardians of the liberties of the country?"

- "It has always been a source of serious reflection and sincere regret with me that the youth of the United States should be sent to foreign countries for the purpose of education. Although there are many who escape the danger of contracting principles unfavorable to republican governments, yet we ought to deprecate the hazard attending ardent and susceptible minds from being too strongly and too early prejudiced in favor of other political systems, before they are capable of appreciating their own."

- "There is nothing which can better deserve your patronage, than the promotion of science and literature. Knowledge is in every country the surest basis of public happiness."

- "The science of figures, to a certain degree, is not only indispensably requisite in every walk of civilised life; but the investigation of mathematical truths accustoms the mind to method and correctness in reasoning, and is an employment peculiarly worthy of rational beings." - Washington in a letter to Nicolas Pike on June 20, 1788.

CHAPTER 2

TANGLING WITH DEATH

After his father died, young George spent most of his time at the family plantation of Mount Vernon, which passed to Lawrence after Augustine died and which would later pass to George. As explained in the previous chapter, it wasn't always an easy life, but it was a life in which young Washington seemed content. George had everything he needed at Mount Vernon, but if he ever wanted to be a great leader, he had to venture out into the outside world.

Then in 1751, at the age of 19, George got his chance when Lawrence arranged a trip down to the Caribbean island of Aruba.

The Washington brothers weren't going there for sun and fun, though—well not exactly, anyway. Lawrence was suffering from tuberculosis, and with no cure for the disease, it was hoped that the sun and warm weather would clear up the respiratory condition. Lawrence also hoped to make some business deals for the family and introduce George to another world.

The trip would prove to be one of the pivotal points in George Washington's life, leaving him scarred, literally.

The Reach of the British Empire

At the time, Aruba was a part of the British Empire, so it was full of British soldiers, sailors, businessmen, colonists, and slaves—*plenty* of slaves. The sugarcane industry was huge in the Caribbean islands in general and Aruba in particular. So, Lawrence hoped to possibly cash in on the booming island's business, but his main priority was getting over his illness.

At 32, Lawrence had a lot of responsibilities. He was married with a child but had lost three children in infancy. He also took care of George and the younger Washington children so he needed to be completely healthy to run things at Mount Vernon.

The Washington boys left Virginia in September 1751 and arrived on the island about a month and a half later. George learned that although he was truly a landlubber, he was also fascinated by the ocean and sea navigation.

George was able to meet a number of people on the island and toured Aruba's many forts, but he contracted smallpox not long after arriving. Smallpox was a potentially deadly virus, especially in the 1700s, causing a high fever, vomiting, and pains in those afflicted. George had a particularly nasty case of smallpox, forcing him to remain in bed for a couple of weeks. The pox that came with the disease also left the left side of his face scarred, which turned out to be a mixed blessing. When George later entered military service, the smallpox scars gave him the look of a seasoned badass, long before he killed his first man.

After all, nothing says "badass" more than facial scars, right?

Washington's bout with smallpox also had an even bigger hidden blessing. Anyone who contracted the virus and lived then developed antibodies that made them immune to it. Later, during the American Revolution, smallpox often decimated both armies and didn't discriminate between officers and enlisted men.

Armies couldn't fight if their generals were laid up with smallpox, but the Continental Army didn't have that disadvantage due to Washington's 1751 bout with the disease in Aruba.

So for George, the Aruba trip had some long-term positive effects; for Lawrence, however, it was an utter failure. The tropics didn't help his TB and about a year later, he succumbed to the disease.

Lawrence's death left a large emotional void in George's life, and it forced him to grow up quickly. George became the head of Mount Vernon and the Washington family; so there were many people who depended upon him. This was the first time that Washington had to put others before himself, and of course, it wouldn't be the last time.

Quotes about Happiness

- "Happiness depends more upon the internal frame of a person's own mind than on the externals in the world." - Letter from Washington to his mother, Mary Washington, on February 15, 1787.
- "[T]he consideration that human happiness and moral duty are inseparably connected, will always continue to prompt me to promote the progress of the former, by inculcating the practice of the latter." - Address from President Washington to the Protestant Episcopal Church on August 19, 1789.
- "Love is said to be an involuntary passion, and it is, therefore, contended that it cannot be resisted. This is true in part only, for like all things else, when nourished and supplied plentifully with ailment, it is rapid in its progress; but let these be withdrawn and it may be stifled in its birth or much stinted in its growth."
- "My anxious recollections, my sympathetic feeling, and my best wishes are irresistibly excited whensoever, in any country, I see an oppressed nation unfurl the banners of freedom."
- "There exists in the economy and course of nature, an indissoluble union between virtue and happiness; between duty and advantage; between the genuine maxims of an honest and magnanimous policy, and the solid rewards of public prosperity and felicity." - Washington's first inaugural speech on April 30, 1789.

CHAPTER 3
A BADASS BUSINESSMAN

Washington wasn't given much time to mourn for his beloved brother. Lawrence's death was certainly a blow to the young and relatively inexperienced George, as he suddenly had the heavy responsibility of being the "man of the house" thrust upon him. George leased Mount Vernon from Lawrence's widow until she died in 1761.

Mount Vernon is a sprawling plantation covering more than 8,000 acres of farmland in Fairfax County, Virginia, which is now part of the Washington, D.C. metro area. In Washington's time, the centerpiece was the mansion, but more than 30 other buildings accompanied it, including barns, sheds, and slaves and servants' quarters.

Back then, Mount Vernon was a living, breathing entity that brought life to hundreds of people in the area through employment and supplied the colonies with plenty of tobacco, hemp, flax, corn, and beans. In order to run the plantation, Washington had to begin thinking like a modern, 18th-century businessman.

Farming is a Tough Gig

The plantation life wasn't always easy for Washington. Many people get the image of Washington and other plantation owners of the era pursuing idle pursuits while their slaves did most of the work. Yes, Washington did own slaves, and in fact, he increased the number he owned to about 100 by the start of the American Revolution. A lot of work went into running such a large operation.

And he wasn't always successful.

The reality is that absentee farm/plantation owners of that era often failed, which Washington nearly found out when he returned home from the French and Indian War in 1858. The plantation had been poorly managed, but after some adjustments, he got things up and running again.

Overall, Washington approached farm work with a scientific mind, which was becoming much more common at the time thanks to the emergence of scientific thinking during the period of Enlightenment. Washington constantly kept up with new farming techniques and technologies and meticulously recorded all profits and losses on the plantation. He did not do this for tax purposes (income tax was still a long way off in the future), but for his own records to see what areas of his plantation needed more, or less, work.

Despite the fact that he ran Mount Vernon with a very modern business approach, Washington is sometimes viewed as a below-average businessman. This assessment isn't fair and is often based on the amount of money that was owed to him that he never collected.

The reality is that Washington was extremely generous with his friends and associates, often giving to them loans with no interest. Also, despite owning several slaves, Washington generally refused to break up families, often costing him money to keep them together.

Still, as a keen businessman and a person who kept on current business practices, Washington diversified Mount Vernon before the Revolution by adding a mill, distillery, and fisheries. By the time the war started, Washington was one of the wealthiest men in Virginia.

Perhaps one of the most badass aspects of Washington's business ventures is that he often did much of the work on the plantation himself. Far from being an absentee landlord, Washington spent much of his presidency at Mount Vernon, working alongside his slaves, servants, and other employees, bringing in crops and making improvements to the mansion and other buildings.

The fact that Washington never considered himself above having to get a little dirty endeared him to Americans—one of the standards used to determine which American presidents are true badasses.

Quotes about Business and Economics

- "Let your discourse with men of business be short and comprehensive."
- "A people... who are possessed of the spirit of commerce, who see and who will pursue their advantages may achieve almost anything." - Washington in a letter to Benjamin Harrison on October 10, 1784.
- "No pecuniary consideration is more urgent, than the regular redemption and discharge of the public debt: on none can delay be more injurious, or an economy of time more valuable. ... Cherish public credit. One method of preserving it is to use it as sparingly as possible: avoiding occasions of expense (and) avoiding likewise the accumulation of debt ... not ungenerously throwing upon posterity the burthen which we ourselves ought to bear."
- "To me, it appears no unjust simile to compare the affairs of this great Continent to the mechanism of a clock, each state representing some one or other of the smaller parts of it which they are endeavoring to put in fine order without considering how useless & unavailing their labor is unless the great Wheel or Spring which is to set the whole in motion is also well attended to & kept in good order." - Washington in a letter to George Mason on March 27, 1779.
- "If ever again our nation stumbles upon unfunded paper, it shall surely be like death to our body politic. This country will crash."

CHAPTER 4

THE THRILL OF WAR

When George returned to Virginia from Aruba, things had changed quite a bit. Lawrence had died, leaving him in charge of the family business, and he abruptly shifted from a relatively carefree young adulthood into being a man with plenty of responsibilities. Washington could have decided that the plantation was his sole focus in life, but he was a civic-minded person and believed that there was more he could do to give back to his community. For this reason, he joined the Virginia militia in 1752.

Now, it should be pointed out that not all badasses of the time joined the military, and not everyone who joined the military was a badass, but in George Washington's case, his military service was central to his badass reputation. Therefore, it's important to understand how it all began.

In addition to young Washington being civic-minded, he was also a typical young man of the era, and most young men in the 1700s wanted to prove themselves on the battlefield. For Washington, that meant potentially fighting Indians on the frontier or possibly the French - or both!

Both would come to pass, but first Washington had to deal with the humdrum of military life in peacetime.

Due to his family's wealth and standing in Virginia society, Lieutenant Governor Robert Dinwiddie assigned George the rank of major and gave him command of a militia district. Washington's unit was basically a bunch of amateur and part-time soldiers, not unlike the National Guard of today, but it was with them that the future president got his first taste of the military and leadership.

Washington immediately took to military life like a fish to water. He enjoyed being posted in the remote regions of the Ohio River valley, as it gave him time to pursue his passion of land surveying, and he proved to be a good leader: His men respected him.

But Washington wouldn't have to wait long to experience what he signed up for—the thrill of war!

QUOTES ON LEADERSHIP

- "Associate with men of good quality if you esteem your own reputation; for it is better to be alone than in bad company."
- "Without Virtue and without integrity the finest talents of the most brilliant accomplishments can never fain the respect or conciliate the esteem of the truly valuable art of mankind." - Washington in a letter to Bartholomew Dandridge on March 8, 1797.
- "Still I hope I shall always possess firmness and virtue enough to maintain (what I consider the most enviable of all titles) the character of an honest man." - Washington in a letter to Alexander Hamilton on August 28, 1788.
- "There is but one straight course, and that is to seek truth and pursue it steadily." - Washington in a letter to Edmund Randolph on July 31, 1795.
- "Few men have virtue to withstand the highest bidder." - Washington in a letter to General Robert Howe on August 17, 1779.

CHAPTER 5

THE ART OF DIPLOMACY

The ancient Chinese philosopher, Sun Tzu, and the early 19th-century German military theorist, Carl von Clausewitz, both wrote that it was best to avoid costly wars. Neither of the two men was a humanitarian, it was just that they believed it made no sense to lose half of your army merely to take a hill. They believed there was also a place for negotiations and for winning the war before the first bullet or arrow was shot.

Any man can kill another man, but it takes a true badass to be a warrior *and* a diplomat.

When George Washington began his service with the Virginia militia, British officials noticed that the young man had a combination of raw intelligence, charisma, and earthy wit. Washington wasn't a stuffy English educated elitist like many of the officers in the British colonial army, even the Americans; instead, he was a true man of the New World.

George Washington could interact with farmers, Indians, and even Frenchmen as well as he could with British aristocrats - even better, sometimes. So, based on these qualities, Washington was chosen for an important mission in 1753. He was to travel with a British contingent to the Northwest (what is now western Pennsylvania) to meet with French and Indian representatives.

The area was described as a "no-man's" land at the time. It was inhabited primarily by different Indian tribes that were often at war with one another, while both the French and British established forts in the area. The French colony of New France (Quebec) was just to the north, on the other side of the St. Lawrence River, while the British settlements of North America remained east of the Appalachian Mountain range.

Washington met with leaders of the Mingo tribe who then brought him to see the French. Although young George got along well with the Indians and French, nothing of consequence was accomplished by the trip, so he returned to Virginia.

Feeling a little let down by the whole endeavor, Washington was pleasantly surprised when Dinwiddie promoted him to colonel and ordered him to raise a small force to return to the Northwest. When Washington was meeting with the Indians and the French, he kept copious notes of their numbers, who their leaders were, and most importantly, their fortifications. The keen intelligence that the British saw in Washington was definitely on display even on this seemingly uneventful trip.

Washington didn't know it at the time, but his first trip to the Northwest would provide the British with valuable intelligence and he would end up being the spark that set off a world-wide war!

INSPIRATIONAL QUOTES BY WASHINGTON

- "Let your heart feel for the afflictions and distress of everyone, and let your hand give in proportion to your purse."
- "Truth will ultimately prevail where pains is taken to bring it to light." - Washington letter to Charles Thurston on August 10, 1794.
- "We should not look back unless it is to derive useful lessons from past errors, and for the purpose of profiting by dearly bought experience."
- "Real men despise battle, but will never run from it."
- "[T]he consideration that human happiness and moral duty are inseparably connected, will always continue to prompt me to promote the progress of the former, by inculcating the practice of the latter." - Washington in an address to the Protestant Episcopal Church on August 19, 1789.

CHAPTER 6

SO BADASS THAT HE STARTED A WAR

Dinwiddie and the British were happy with Washington's efforts in the Northwest, but they had bigger plans for the young officer. They also had bigger plans for the region, as well as the French and the Indians living there.

As Washington was returning from Pennsylvania, Dinwiddie sent a fur trader and militia officer named William Trent to build a fort in the area that would later become Pittsburgh.

The French and their Indian allies expelled Trent and his men from the area. When Washington heard about the events in April 1754, he marched with a small force of Virginians to meet the Mingo Indian chief Tanacharison and show the French how well a Virginian unit could fight.

Washington probably didn't know it at the time, but his actions in the late spring and early summer of that year would mark the beginning of the French and Indian War (1754-1763), which was the opening stage of the worldwide Seven Years' War (1756-1763)

Fighting the French

The French and Indian War is only really known by that name in the United States. The rest of the world considers it just to be the North American theater of the Seven Years' War. But it was an important war nonetheless, and our boy George was basically the reason it started.

When you consider that Washington was many years away from becoming a rebel leader, never mind the president, and he ended up starting a world war, you have to admit that he's pretty much a badass.

The truth is, though, that war between the British and French was probably bound to happen regardless of Washington's actions. The British were pushing west, over the Appalachian Mountains, establishing small settlements as they went. Most of the Indian tribes didn't like the development, but the British authorities were able to make an alliance with the Iroquois Confederation.

The French also didn't like it. Unlike the British, the French weren't attempting to colonize Pennsylvania, instead preferring to establish trading posts. Most of the Indians in the region therefore preferred the French.

On the global scale, by that time, the British had aligned with Prussia, Portugal, and some smaller German-speaking principalities, while the French had the Russians, Swedes, and Spanish in their camp.

Washington and Tanacharison and their men ambushed a French military unit led by Joseph Coulon de Jumonville on May 28, 1754. The attack probably left all of the approximately 35 French soldiers' dead and put Washington in a tough position, leaving him with only two options. He could either retreat back into British territory or stand his ground and wait for reinforcements.

Washington decided to do the latter.

In early June, Washington ordered a hastily-built fortification, which became known as Fort Necessity. Although a good idea, the fort was really more for show than anything and unfortunately for Washington, no reinforcements arrived. In fact, Tanacharison and most of the Indian allies abandoned the fort.

The French eventually attacked with an overwhelming force, which forced Washington to surrender it on July 3.

Here's where things get more interesting.

As part of the surrender, the French made Washington sign a document whereby he essentially admitted to assassinating de Jumonville. With that signature, Washington started the French and Indian War, which in turn set off the Seven Years' War. Despite labelling him a war criminal, the French went on to release Washington to fight more battles in the war.

The truth is, they probably thought the young officer was more of a hindrance to the British than anything.

Still, Washington acquitted himself quite well for the remainder of the war. He learned a great deal about military tactics, the terrain of North American, and he also made invaluable connections that he later used in the American Revolution.

But you have to admit, it's pretty badass that George Washington started the French and Indian War—unknowingly and unintentionally!

Quotes about War

- "Discipline is the soul of an army. It makes small numbers formidable; procures success to the weak, and esteem to all."
- "First in war, first in peace, and first in the hearts of his countrymen." – Henry Lee, a former soldier of Washington's, on George Washington.
- "To place any dependence upon militia, is, assuredly, resting upon a broken staff."
- "To be prepared for war is one of the most effectual means of preserving peace." –
- Washington's first address to Congress as president on January 8, 1790.
- "Over grown military establishments are under any form of government inauspicious to liberty, and are to be regarded as particularly hostile to republican liberty."

CHAPTER 7

WASHINGTON WAS A LATE BLOOMER

When George returned home from the French and Indian War in 1758, he was 26, single, and ready to mingle. Well, not really. The dating scene in the 1700s wasn't like what it is today, to say the least, and young Washington really wasn't all that interested in settling down. The war had opened up plenty of new opportunities for young George and he was ready to take them.

One option he considered was a fulltime career in the British army.

Secondly, he was approached by leaders in Virginia to run for the House of Burgess, which was the name of Virginia's elected assembly of the time.

Lastly, he also could have chosen to focus on real estate. The governor had promised lands west of the Appalachian Mountains to all militia members who had fought in the French and Indian War. He also could have dedicated himself to expanding Mount Vernon's size and scope.

Or he could've done all of these.

As we'll see later, the first possibility became a problem because Washington just "wasn't British enough." Obviously, on the second option, Washington did pursue a political career later. He also did expand his land holdings, partially by claiming the reward the governor offered to militia members and partially through marriage.

On January 6, 1759, Washington married the 27-year-old widow, Martha Dandridge Custis. George was kind of a late bloomer by the era's standards, but he was just waiting for the right girl. Martha brought plenty of land, slaves, and money to the marriage from her first marriage, so Washington was able to increase his real estate holdings immensely. She also brought two children, John and Martha (Patsy), from her previous marriage, whom Washington raised as his own.

Martha and George never had children of their own.

The reason for this remains a historical mystery. Some historians argue that Martha was unable to after the difficult birth of Patsy, while others believe that Washington was left sterile from smallpox.

Whatever the reason, by all accounts, the couple was happy. Martha was a grounding force for Washington, who sometimes let emotions get the better of him. As Washington made his badass climb through military and politics, Martha, John, and Patsy were there every step of the way to support him.

Without his family's support, George Washington probably wouldn't have been half the badass that he was.

Quotes on Friends and Family

- "I never did, nor do I believe I ever shall, give advice to a woman who is setting out on a matrimonial voyage; first, because I never could advise one to marry without her own consent; and, secondly, I know it is to no purpose to advise her to refrain when she has obtained it. A woman very rarely asks an opinion or requires advice on such an occasion, till her resolution is formed; and then it is with the hope and expectation of obtaining a sanction, not that she means to be governed by your disapprobation, that she applies." - George Washington in a letter to his cousin, Lund Washington, on September 20, 1783, about the potential marriage of his stepdaughter, Patsy.
- "My mother was the most beautiful woman I ever saw. All I am I owe to my mother."
- "True friendship is a plant of slow growth, and must undergo and withstand the shocks of adversity, before it is entitled to the appellation."
- "Since the death of my father four years ago, our lives have become difficult, and I must help my family."
- "Be courteous to all, but intimate with few, and let those few be well tried before you give them your confidence."

CHAPTER 8

A TOWERING PRESENCE

Every epic badass in world history is known for his or her engaging, persuasive personality, and often an equally impressive physical stature to go along with it. In George Washington's case, everyone immediately took note when he entered a room because in addition to his natural charisma, he had a physical presence that definitely grabbed attention and could be downright intimidating.

Washington stood about 6'0 to 6'4 in height, although his precise height will probably never be known due to a lack of records that definitively state as much and no photography at the time. Either way, Washington was tall for the era; taller than most men he worked with and commanded.

Of course, this would later be important when he dealt with stubborn Patriot politicians, recalcitrant officers, and especially, the French. But we'll get to all of that in due time.

Washington was said to have an average to athletic build, which he built from working on Mount Vernon all his life. Remember, Washington may have been born to privilege, but he was a true American who didn't mind getting his hands dirty.

George had light-blue eyes and auburn hair, but most people didn't know that because he usually wore a powdered wig like most men of status did during the 1700s. Overall, he was considered by many to be handsome, although due to the scars from his bout with smallpox, he'd be considered a bit unconventionally handsome by today's standards.

Always aware of himself and his peers, Washington accentuated his height by practicing good posture, shaking hands firmly, and always looking in the eyes of those he spoke to. Those who met Washington always remembered the encounter. George Washington clearly knew how to use his physical presence to win over a room, influence his opponents, and get every last drop of effort from his men on the battlefield.

If that isn't badass, I don't know what is.

Quotes about Ethics and Integrity

- "Let us raise a standard to which the wise and honest can repair; the rest is in the hands of God."
- "The best and only safe road to honor, glory, and true dignity is justice." – Washington letter to the Marquis de LaFayette on September 30, 1779.
- "Integrity and firmness is all I can promise; these, be the voyage long or short, never shall forsake me though I be deserted by all men. For of the consolations which are to be derived from these (under any circumstances) the world cannot deprive me." –
- Washington in a letter to Henry Knox on April 1, 1789.
- "Honesty will be found on every experiment, to be the best and only true policy; let us then as a Nation be just."
- "Where is the man to be found who wishes to remain indebted for the defense of his own person and property to the exertions, the bravery, and the blood of others, without making one generous effort to repay the debt of honor and gratitude?"

CHAPTER 9

GETTING PASSED OVER

George always knew that he wasn't a true Brit. He never really claimed to be British either - among colonials, he often wore the fact that he wasn't British educated as a badge of honor to some extent. On the one hand, he was keenly aware that British born and raised people often looked down upon him for his lack of a British education, but on the other hand, he knew that a classical British education did little for success in the New World.

With that said, Washington did desire to be accepted among Britain's military elite.

When Washington served in the French and Indian War, he got the "military bug" and a bit of the "war fever."

Washington decided that he wanted to be a career military man and above all, to wear the famed "red coat" of a British officer. But unfortunately for Washington, that ambush he led on the French in Pennsylvania kept coming back to haunt him. It definitely looked bad and was a source of embarrassment for the British, who although engaged in a bloody war with the French, would never want to be accused of being ungentlemanly.

But even worse for Washington, he found out that there just wasn't any place for Americans in the British army. This rejection and the way it unfolded went far in shaping Washington's attitude toward the British and his image as a rebellious badass.

Riding with Braddock

British General Edward Braddock arrived in Virginia in 1755 with a plan to overwhelm the French and their Indian allies with superior British arms and tactics. Washington was one of the first notable "colonials" - as Americans were often referred to at the time - to volunteer his services, but he was immediately met with a cold attitude. He learned that although he could join the expedition, he could only do so as a "provincial officer," which meant that he was technically outranked by *all* British officers.

Needless to say, Washington didn't have time for all that business.

So, always thinking, George came up with a way to take part in the expedition with his pride intact. He volunteered his services to Braddock as an unpaid aide, which meant that he didn't have to take lower-ranking British officers' abuse, and he could offer his knowledge of the region to Braddock.

Well, that's how it was supposed to work, anyway.

But as the expedition got to Pennsylvania, Washington quickly learned that his knowledge of the terrain, climate, and Indians of the Northwest meant very little to Braddock and the other British officers. To them, Washington was just another colonial yokel.

But Washington would have the last laugh.

On July 9, 1755, Braddock and 1,300 of his men met a slightly smaller force of French militia and Indians at the Battle of Monongahela, about ten miles east of modern Pittsburgh.

The battle was more of a massacre than anything, with 457 of the British killed and more than 450 wounded. General Braddock was among those who died, but young Washington rallied the troops on his trusty white horse.

In fact, Washington is said to have stalled the French and Indian advance, allowing the British to take their wounded off the battlefield.

As for George, his pride may have been initially wounded by the British after being passed over for promotion, but he dealt with the situation like a true badass. He fought like a hero on the battlefield and despite the loss continued to serve with honor in the war. When he returned to Virginia after the war, he went back to plantation life and later politics, believing that his military career was long behind him.

But, of course, some major historical events eventually brought him back to the military.

QUOTES ON PERSEVERANCE

- "We must never despair; our situation has been compromising before, and it has changed for the better; so I trust it will again. If difficulties arise, we must put forth new exertion and proportion our efforts to the exigencies of the times." - Washington in a letter to General Philip Schuyler on July 15, 1777.
- "But as it has been a kind of destiny, that has thrown me upon this service, I shall hope that my undertaking it is designed to answer some good purpose."
- "One of the difficulties in bringing about change in an organization is that you must do so through the persons who have been most successful in that organization, no matter how faulty the system or the organization is. To such persons, you see, it is the best of all possible organizations, because look who was selected by it and look who succeeded most in it. Yet, these are the very people through whom we must bring about improvements."
- "Perseverance and spirit have done wonders in all ages."
- "Ours is a kind of struggle designed, I dare say, by Providence to try the patience, fortitude, and virtue of men. None, therefore, who is engaged in it, will suffer himself, I trust, to sink under difficulties, or be discouraged by hardships. If he cannot do as he wishes, he must do what he can." - Washington in a letter to Andrew Lewis on October 15, 1778.

CHAPTER 10

BECOMING A BADASS REVOLUTIONARY LEADER

By 1767, George Washington was living a very good life by any standard of the time. He had a nice family, was financially wealthy from his plantation and business deals, had an excellent reputation from his service in the French and Indian War, and was a respected member of the Virginia House of Burgesses. Many people would have simply rested on their laurels and enjoyed life.

But Washington was constantly driven to prove himself and do more.

And by the 1760s, the situation had changed dramatically in the 13 American Colonies. The Stamp Act of 1765 was the first major tax by the British on the American colonials. The Americans despised it because they had no say over it. They had no input because they weren't allowed any members in the British Parliament.

Americans began protesting the tax, saying, "No taxation without representation!"

Virginia and Massachusetts became the two hotbeds of resistance and protest, yet Washington stayed out of the initial fray. It wasn't that Washington was against the protests - he wasn't - or that he had any love for the British - he didn't - but if you remember, George Washington was known for his *practical* intelligence. He decided to sit on the sidelines for a bit and see how things played out.

Finally, in 1767, the British made up Washington's mind for him when they passed a series of taxes and duties known collectively as the Townshend Act.

George Becomes a Patriot

The Townshend Act led to a fresh wave of protests across the American colonies and eventually, leaders emerged who organized the discontent into a coherent movement known as the Patriot movement. The Patriots didn't immediately call for independence from Britain, but most of the notable leaders, including Washington, believed that it was inevitable.

When the Boston Tea Party - a protest by the Sons of Liberty against the British Tea Act - took place in 1773, the British responded by passing the so-called Intolerable Act on the American colonies. The Intolerable Act included a number of laws that took even more power from the colonial governments and forced them to house British troops.

It was too much for most Patriot leaders, including Washington.

At the age of 42, George Washington had come into his own as a political and military leader. When the Patriots of the American colonies decided to form their own government called the Continental Congress, Washington was elected as one of Virginia's delegates.

But George knew that his place would be on the battlefield. As much as speech-making and theoretical writing were important for the Patriot movement, Washington knew that another Virginian, Thomas Jefferson, was better suited for that duty. George knew that if their movement had any chance of surviving, it would only happen on the battlefield.

Washington began organizing and training local militias, but he realized they could only serve in a support role if war broke out with Britain. The Americans had to have a truly professional, standing army if they hoped to win.

After the Battles of Lexington and Concord in April 1775, the Continental Congress decided to choose a general from among their ranks to form and lead the Continental Army. Future president John Adams nominated Washington, and the vote was unanimous in his favor.

Although George hadn't lobbied for the position, he dutifully accepted and immediately got to work creating a professional army out of a motley collection of farmers, merchants, sailors, and militia.

Quotes about Resistance and Revolution

- "Our conflict is not likely to cease so soon as every good man would wish. The measure of inequity is not yet filled—and unless we can return a little more to first principles, & act a little more upon patriotic ground, I do not know when it will—or—what may be the issue of the contest—Speculation—peculation—engrossing—forestalling—with all their concomitants, afford too many melancholy proofs of the decay of public virtue; and too glaring instances of its being the interest & desire of too many, who would wish to be thought friends, to continue the War." - Washington in a letter to James Warren on March 31, 1779.
- "The Stamp Act imposed on the colonies by the Parliament of Great Britain is an ill-judged measure. Parliament has no right to put its hands into our pockets without our consent."
- "A people contending for life and liberty are seldom disposed to look with a favorable eye upon either men or measures whose passions, interests or consequences will clash with those inestimable objects."
- "It is yet to be decided whether the Revolution must ultimately be considered as a blessing or a curse: a blessing or a curse, not to the present age alone, for with our fate will the destiny of unborn millions be involved."

– Washington in a circular to the states upon the completion of the American Revolution in 1783.

- "Remember, officers and soldiers, that you are fighting for the blessings of liberty."

CHAPTER 11

THE NATION'S FIRST GENERAL

Before we explore how Washington molded a bunch of farmers, merchants, and militia into the Continental Army, it's important to understand what he had to deal with due to his decision to lead the Continentals.

Of course, Washington had to cope with privations on the frontlines, especially when the Continentals were camped at Valley Forge. He also put his life on the line whenever he led his men into battle. He was truly a man who led by example and was always at the front with his men.

Yes, Washington faced all the usual problems and pressures that came with leading an army into war, but on top of that, he knew that losing the war would probably cost him his life.

Many in the British Parliament called for Washington's arrest, trial, and execution after he lost the war. Yes, they put it in those terms, even though the war had just begun. Nearly all of the British people, even those who sympathized with the Patriots, were pretty complacent and believed that the colonists didn't stand a chance against the mighty British Army.

Washington was also targeted by an assassination plot in 1776, so he certainly had good reason to believe that, if his forces lost the war, he'd probably lose his life. So what impact did all this have on Washington and the Revolution? Well, it's situations like this that tend to "separate the men from the boys" as they say, or in our case, the average person from the badasses.

And in true badass nature, George Washington didn't let the threats to his life hold him back. If anything, they appear to have made him more determined to fight the British.

QUOTES ON LEADERSHIP

- "It is much to be wished that public faith may be held inviolate—Painful is it even in thought that attempts should be made to weaken the bands of it. It is a dangerous experiment—once slacken the reins and the power is lost—and it is questionable with me whether the advocates of the measure foresee all the consequences of it. It is an old adage that honesty is the best policy—this applies to public as well as private life—to States as well as individuals." - Washington in a letter to James Madison on November 30, 1785.
- "At present, my time is so much taken up at my Desk, that I am obliged to neglect many other essential parts of my Duty; it is absolutely necessary therefore for me to have person's that can think for me, as well as execute Orders—This it is that pains me, when I think of Mr White's expectation of coming into my Family, if an opening happens. I can derive no earthly assistance from such a Man—and my friend Baylor is much such another. Although as good, and as obliging a person as any in the World." - Washington in a letter to Colonel Joseph Reed on January 23, 1776.
- "Discipline is the soul of an army. It makes small numbers formidable; procures success to the weak, and esteem to all."
- "Leadership is not only having a vision, but also having the courage, the discipline, and the resources to get you there."

- “The foolish and wicked practice of profane cursing and swearing...is a vice so mean and low, without any temptation, that every man of sense and character detests and despises it.”

CHAPTER 12

WHIPPING THE ARMY INTO SHAPE

First thing's first: In order to effectively fight a war, you have to have at least the appearance of an army. When Washington took over in 1775, what he had before him was anything but.

Sure, there were some enthusiastic guys signing up to kick some British butt, and a good share of them even knew how to shoot quite well and live off the land if need be. And more than a few of the men who would comprise the officer corps had combat experience from the French and Indian War.

With that said, in 1775, the Continental Army was far from being a formidable army.

All of this makes Washington's eventual victory even that much more badass. Somehow, in some way, George Washington was able to take a band of farmers with no military experience and mold them into an army capable of defeating the greatest military machine the world had seen. Much of Washington's success came from his battlefield tactics and strategies, and France's entry into the war played a major role, but none of that would have been possible if the

General hadn't whipped the Continental Army into shape in the first few months of its existence.

The Empire on Which the Sun Never Sets

To understand what Washington was up against and how his victory was so incredible, it's important to briefly take a look at the British Empire. Beginning in the 1500s, the British decided that they would expand beyond their borders and conquer lands in the newly-discovered Americas as well as in Africa and Asia. The Spanish, Portuguese, Dutch, and French also had this idea, so the British needed to build a state of the art military to contend with the other European powers.

And since Britain is an island nation, they developed the greatest navy in the history of the world.

By the time of the American Revolution, the British controlled about one-quarter of the world's land, which earned the British Empire the nickname, "the Empire on which the Sun never sets."

So when the American Patriots made the decision to finally fight the British, it was a bold move, to say the least.

Washington had to build an army from the ground up, which he did by taking men from the various colonial militias. He immediately saw that victory could only be achieved—and the army would only survive—if it were organized, so he structured the Continental Army into three divisions, six brigades, and 38 regiments.

A new *esprit de corps* was also given to the army. The men of the Continental Army, officers and enlisted, were repeatedly told they were fighting for *all* of the colonies, not just the ones they came from. This would prove crucial to uniting the colonies during the war – and again after they were building the new nation.

Washington also had to work on logistics, stamp out rivalries among his officers, and get the men to even *look* like a proper army before they went on the battlefield. And he had to do it quickly because the British occupied Boston after the Battle of Lexington and Concord.

It came as a shock to many throughout the world when Washington led the successful siege of Boston that vanquished the British from New England on March 17, 1776. Although the siege of Boston was a clear victory for Washington and proved to the British that he was a true badass that should not be taken lightly, it was the last victory he would see in a while.

Quotes on Patriotism

- "I beg you, at the same time, to do me the justice to be assured that this resolution has not been taken without a strict regard to all the considerations appertaining to the relation which binds a dutiful citizen to his country." - Washington's 1796 Farewell Address to the nation.
- "The name of American, which belongs to you, in your national capacity, must always exalt the just pride of Patriotism."
- "My ardent desire is, and my aim has been, to comply strictly with all our engagements, foreign and domestic, but to keep the United States free from political connections with every other country; to see that they may be independent of all and under the influence of none."
- "Our country's honor calls upon us for a vigorous and manly exertion; and if we now shamefully fail, we shall become infamous to the whole world."
- "Excessive partiality for one foreign nation and excessive dislike of another cause those whom they actuate to see danger only on one side, and serve to veil and even second the arts of influence on the other. Real patriots who may resist the intrigues of the favorite are liable to become suspected and odious, while its tools and dupes usurp the applause and confidence of the people, to surrender their interests." - Washington's 1796 Farewell Address to the nation.

CHAPTER 13

LOSING THE BIG APPLE

After vanquishing the British from Boston, the Patriots were on a high. Many thought that the war was all but over, and the British would come to an agreement on the Patriots terms. When that didn't happen, Thomas Jefferson wrote 'The Declaration of Independence', which was signed by all of the leaders in Philadelphia - and the rest, as they say, was history.

All of that was great, but it didn't mean much for George Washington. He knew that America's independence could only truly be won on the battlefield. With that said, Washington was often at the whims of the non-military and highly political Continental Congress. Like the badass that he was, Washington sometimes ignored them, but it was impossible to do so all the time. After all, Congress paid for the Army, when and if they did actually pay, and Washington was also smart enough to know that he was fighting a political and cultural war as much as it was a standard, conventional war.

So when the Continental Congress talked, Washington at least had to listen.

George had the idea of bringing the war to the British by invading Quebec and possibly getting the French-Canadians to join them. The Congress had other ideas, though.

The Congress ordered Washington to defend New York City and Long Island. At that time, New York City was only Manhattan—the other boroughs were independent cities. It proved to be a gargantuan task that Washington was basically set up to fail. Washington had less than 20,000 men against British General William Howe's more than 30,000 men. The area was extremely vast and much of it rural (yes, that's hard to believe considering modern NYC), and worst of all, Washington had little to no intelligence network.

The people of Long Island were also notoriously Torrie (loyalist) at the time.

Rising above Defeat

The British fleet arrived on the shores of what is now Brooklyn on August 22, sailing over the narrows from what is now Staten Island. General Howe had offered Washington a pardon for his crimes against the British crown, but Washington replied that since no crimes had been committed by him or anyone on his side, there was no reason for a pardon.

General Howe wasn't amused.

So the main British force of about 20,000 men marched from the shore inland to engage Washington's force of about 10,000 men who were dug into fortifications in the heights of Brooklyn.

The Continentals fought bravely during the Battle of Long Island on August 27, but they were overwhelmed by the British forces and forced to retreat back into New York City. As the British approached the city, though, Washington ordered a total retreat of the Continental forces all the way to the capital city of Philadelphia.

The Battle of Long Island was a demoralizing defeat for many Patriots, especially the Patriots who didn't understand warfare. Their hopes of a quick war were dashed and many began to question Washington's leadership abilities.

But those who had a military background knew that defeating the largest and most efficient military machine in the world wouldn't be easy and it would come with its fair share of losses. Washington knew that the war would be a demonstration of tenacity: the tenacity of Americans in general, the tenacity of his army, and most importantly, his own tenacity. It was during the Continental Army's march to Philadelphia when Washington first displayed his strategy of tenacity.

You see, as anxiety on the Patriot side began to spread among those with no military background, it also spread among the British. The British were glad they won the Battle of Long Island, but they were more upset they didn't capture Washington. They knew capturing Washington was their key to winning the war and as long as he was free with his army, there was a chance he could defeat them.

Or at least, not lose to them.

And that's pretty much what Washington's early military strategy boiled down to - just don't lose to the British. Sure, winning battles was great, but as long as the Continental Army remained intact and on the field, then the British could not win. And if the British weren't winning, it meant that the Patriots *were* winning.

That right there is what made George Washington such as badass general. He realized that the American Revolution was a new kind of war unlike most that had been fought in Europe in recent years. It was part conventional war, but it was also part asymmetrical. Washington took everything he learned in the French and Indian War, including what he learned from his Indian allies and enemies, and applied it to fighting the British.

Washington didn't need to beat the British to defeat them necessarily; he only needed to bleed them to the point where keeping their army on the field was no longer economically feasible - or politically popular back in England.

Quotes on Tenacity and Overcoming Failure

- "But Patience is a noble Virtue, and when rightly exercised, does not fail of its Reward." – Washington in a letter to John Rodgers on June 11, 1783.
- "We must never despair; our situation has been compromising before, and it has changed for the better; so I trust it will again. If difficulties arise, we must put forth new exertion and proportion our efforts to the exigencies of the times." – Washington in a letter to General Schuyler on July 15, 1777.
- "It is too probable that no plan we propose will be adopted. Perhaps another dreadful conflict is to be sustained. If, to please the people, we offer what we ourselves disprove, how can we afterwards defend our work? Let us raise a standard to which the wise and the honest can repair. The event is in the hand of God."
- "The ways of Providence being inscrutable, and the justice of it not to be scanned by the shallow eye of humanity, nor to be counteracted by the utmost efforts of human power or wisdom, resignation, and as far as the strength of our reason and religion can carry us, a cheerful acquiescence to the Divine Will, is what we are to aim." – Washington in a letter to Colonel Bassett on April 20, 1773.
- "As an encouragement to which we have opened the fertile plains of the Ohio to the poor, the needy and the

oppressed of the Earth; any one therefore who is heavy laden, or who wants land to cultivate, may repair thither and abound, as in the Land of promise, with milk and honey: the ways are preparing, and the roads will be made easy, thro' the channels of Potomac and James river."

CHAPTER 14

CROSSING THE DELAWARE LIKE A BOSS

At some point in your life, you've no doubt seen Emanuel Leutze's famous painting, *Washington Crossing the Delaware*. I mean, how can you possibly forget it: Washington is standing on an overloaded dinghy overlooking the frozen Delaware River as he and his men cross, ready to strike the Hessians in New Jersey.

The 1851 painting helped cement Washington's reputation as a badass, but it wasn't entirely true.

Washington did in fact cross the Delaware River, and he did lead a successful assault on the German mercenaries, known as Hessians, who were fighting for the British. But we really don't know if he stood on the prow of the boat as depicted in the painting. Remember, this was long before photography and even Leutze's well-known picture wasn't completed until nearly 80 years after the event when everyone who was there was long dead.

Based on what we know about Washington, though, he probably did stand there like that. I mean that would be pretty fitting for a badass, right?

But as badass as that image is, everything Washington did just before and right after that point was even more badass.

Finding Hope

By late 1776, things looked pretty bleak for Washington, the Continental Army, and the Patriots in general. The Continental Army was divided literally and figuratively, with part of it north of New York City and Washington and the main part in Pennsylvania. To make matters worse, Continental General Charles Lee was captured by the British in New Jersey.

Throughout America and even in the Continental camp, people were wondering if Congress should appoint a new general.

To top things off, the Continental Army men weren't being paid, they were under-supplied and many were not re-enlisting or even deserting.

Washington knew that the only thing that could keep the cause going and the army together was to win a quick, decisive victory. The way the British were amassed, there was little hope of defeating them in a straight-up battle, at least one that wouldn't cost Washington half his army. So, Washington waited and waited for inspiration.

And then it happened!

George received an intelligence report from his spy network (we'll get to them in a bit) stating that a company of German mercenaries from the kingdoms of Hesse-Cassel and Hesse-Hanau—which is why they were called Hessians - were camped just across the Delaware River in Trenton, New Jersey.

Washington decided to lead a force of about 2,500 across the river on Christmas Day night to surprise the Germans the next morning. Just as he thought, the Hessians were in no condition to fight on the 26th due to the copious amounts of beer, ham, and sauerkraut they had consumed at Christmas.

The Continentals only killed 22 Hessians, but they took over 800 prisoners and only had two men who died, both from frostbite. It was certainly a master strategic stroke, which earned Washington the begrudging respect of the British.

With that said, the British did try to downplay the American victory at Trenton as strategically unimportant and over an enemy that was not too interested in fighting. Although there is some truth to these statements, Washington's success at Trenton revived the hopes of Patriots across the colonies. Washington proved to the Americans he wasn't done and that he had plenty of fight left in him. More importantly, he proved to the French that he was a true badass who could take a licking and keep on ticking.

Quotes on Freedom

- "The time is now near at hand which must probably determine whether Americans are to be freemen or slaves; whether they are to have any property they can call their own; whether their houses and farms are to be pillaged and destroyed, and themselves consigned to a state of wretchedness from which no human efforts will deliver them." -
- Washington's address to the Continental Army before the Battle of Long Island on August 27, 1776.
- "A free people ought not only to be armed but disciplined; to which end a Uniform and well digested plan is requisite: And their safety and interest require that they should promote such manufactories, as tend to render them independent on others, for essential, particularly for military supplies." - Washington's State of the Union Address on January 8, 1790.
- "Liberty, when it begins to take root, is a plant of rapid growth."
- "The preservation of the sacred fire of liberty, and the destiny of the Republican model of Government, are justly considered as deeply, perhaps as finally staked, on the experiment entrusted to the hands of the American people."
- "Arbitrary power is most easily established on the ruins of liberty abused to licentiousness." - Washington in a circular to the state on June 8, 1783.

CHAPTER 15

MAKING IT THROUGH LEAN TIMES

After Washington whipped the Hessians at Trenton and defeated General Howe and the British in smaller battles in New Jersey, it looked like the Patriots had the advantage. Maybe the war was close to an end? Maybe the British were willing to come to terms and allow the Americans independence?

Think again.

It was much too soon in 1777 for the British to imagine giving up. With that said, though, they did begin to realize that George Washington was much more than just a country yokel who got lucky a couple of times. Many at the top of the British command began to see Washington as a "sly fox" that needed to be "bagged." Although most generals of the time would have probably rather been compared to a lion or a wolf, Washington wasn't too proud to be likened to a fox.

After all, foxes are cunning predators that are rarely seen and often evade capture, even when dozens of dogs are employed to catch them.

Howe had his best chance to catch the American fox when he caught up to him and the Continental Army just south of

Philadelphia at a place called Brandywine on September 11, 1777.

Not only did Washington's force lose at Brandywine, but they suffered heavy casualties, with 250 killed, 600 wounded, and 400 captured. The Continental Congress had to evacuate Philadelphia to the British and the Continental Army had to basically go into hiding for the winter of 1777-1778.

It was perhaps the lowest point in the war for Washington.

Definitely Not a Fun Camp

Washington led the Continental Army to a location just northwest of Philadelphia to a place that would become known as Valley Forge. Today, Valley Forge is associated with not only the birth of America but the very gritty essence of Americans.

But for that winter, it was truly an awful place.

The troops weren't paid and they were underfed, under-supplied, and living through a cold Pennsylvania winter. Frostbite, dysentery, and smallpox ravaged the camp, and desertions were commonplace.

There were also rumblings within the camp of a planned coup against Washington and most of the general's high command were also fighting among themselves.

All of this made surviving the winter at Valley Forge Washington's greatest battle.

The camp was so-called because there was an iron forge there before the war. There were also supplies held there, but the British took what they could before the Continental Army arrived, which made the winter that much more difficult. To make things worse, the Continental Army had most of its supply lines cut off by the British, so very few things could come in and out of Valley Forge.

The Americans did have "fire cakes" to eat!

You're no doubt wondering, "What are fire cakes?"

Well, fire cakes are made by taking some flour, mixing it with some water, and then putting the clump on a hot rock from a fire to "cook" it. The result was something that had no taste, was barely edible, and more often than not giving the person who ate it a bad case of diarrhea!

Washington just had to keep the troops together through the winter to give them a chance, hoping that perhaps some type of miracle would happen.

And then one did happen, sort of.

One thing that all badasses throughout history share is a fair amount of luck. Sure, badasses tend to be more intelligent and have more charisma than the average person, but they also have an intangible ability to have things go their way at the right moment. Of course, most of us call that luck.

Washington's big lucky break came on February 6, 1778 when the French signed a military alliance with the Americans. Without French support, the Americans probably couldn't have won the war. To Washington's credit, the French only joined the alliance when they saw that Washington was a true badass capable of defeating the British on the battlefield.

By the time the ice at Valley Forge began to thaw in March, things looked good again for Washington and the Continental Army.

QUOTES ABOUT THE MILITARY

- "It may be laid down as a primary position, and the basis of our system, that every Citizen who enjoys the protection of a free Government, owes not only a proportion of his property, but even his personal services to the defence of it, and consequently that the Citizens of America (with a few legal and official exceptions) from 18 to 50 Years of Age should be borne on the Militia Rolls, provided with uniform and arms, and so far accustomed to the use of them, that the Total strength of the Country might be called forth at a Short Notice on any very interesting Emergency." - Washington in a letter to Alexander Hamilton on May 2, 1783.
- "To place any dependance upon Militia, is, assuredly, resting upon a broken staff. Men just dragged from the tender Scenes of domestick life—unaccustomed to the din of Arms—totally unacquainted with every kind of Military skill, which being followed by a want of Confidence in themselves when opposed to Troops regularly trained—disciplined, and appointed—superior in knowledge, & superior in Arms, makes them timid, and ready to fly from their own Shadows. Besides, the sudden change in their manner of living (particularly in the lodging) brings on sickness in many; impatience in all; & such an unconquerable desire of returning to their respective homes that it not only produces shameful, & scandalous Desertions among themselves, but infuses the

like spirit in others—Again, Men accustomed to unbounded freedom, and no control, cannot brooke the Restraint which is indispensably necessary to the good Order and Government of an Army." - Washington in a letter to John Hancock on September 25, 1776.

- "It follows then as certain as that night succeeds the day, that without a decisive naval force we can do nothing definitive, and with it, everything honorable and glorious."
- "When we assumed the Soldier, we did not lay aside the Citizen."
- "Another matter highly worthy of attention is, that other rules and regulations may be adopted for the government of the army, than those now in existence; otherwise the army, but for the name, might as well be disbanded." - Washington's address to the Continental Congress about the state of the Continental Army on September 24, 1776.

CHAPTER 16

USING A BADASS SPY RING

There were a lot of factors that made George Washington a successful, badass general, but perhaps one of the most important was his forward-thinking attitude. He understood that although the American Revolution was a war that employed many of the old, standard paradigms of warfare, it was also a new type of war.

The term "asymmetrical warfare" can refer to any type of warfare that doesn't fit the standard type of conventional warfare. When the American minutemen fought the British at Lexington and Concord, they used asymmetrical warfare, as did many other Patriots across the colonies. Instead of lining up in tight lines to get shot by the British, they decided that sniper shots from the trees and hit-and-run tactics would be more successful.

Although Washington's Continental Army fought the British on the battlefield following standard warfare rules of the time, Washington knew that no matter how hard his men fought, he probably needed an extra edge.

Washington believed that New York was the key to American victory or defeat. He thought that the longer the British held New York, the harder it would be for American victory.

Washington also knew that New York was the nerve center of British military activities in America: Most of the troops were stationed there and all of the high ranking officers made it their temporary homes.

With all of that in mind, Washington decided to put a man on the "inside."

You're probably thinking it would have been easy to find a willing Patriot spy in New York, but that just wasn't the case. New York was a stronghold of loyalist activity and anyone caught spying for the Patriots faced certain death.

And that's what happened to Washington's first spy, Nathan Hale.

Nathan Hale was Washington's first guy on the inside, but he was betrayed by a source, captured, and executed on September 22, 1776.

It was a serious setback for Washington's intelligence efforts, but true badasses aren't so easily deterred, so George went back to the drawing board.

The Culper Spy Ring

Washington didn't have to wait long for another opportunity. Washington learned that one of his young officers, Major Benjamin Tallmadge, who ran reconnaissance, was the key to his intelligence problems. Tallmadge was a Long Island native who kept in contact with many of his old friends who just happened to be secret Patriots.

Friends like Abraham Woodhull and Anna Strong.

Once Washington gave the go-ahead for the ring, Continental Army lieutenant Caleb Brewster, who was also a Long Island native, acted as the courier for the group, picking up intelligence from dead drops throughout Long Island. Woodhull and Strong eventually recruited more spies into the ring, including a New York City tavern owner named Robert Townshend.

Washington's generals fought him tooth and nail on funding the ring, arguing that true gentleman should never employ such underhanded methods during wartime. The ironic truth is that the British also had an elaborate spy ring, and they had no qualms about looking like gentlemen - they did whatever they could to gather intelligence on the Continental Army.

Once again, Washington was proved right and his critics had to eat crow. The Culper spy ring played a major role in the American Revolution and may have given the Patriots an edge. Here is just a partial list of some of the things this badass spy ring did.

They learned of the Hessian camp at Trenton and alerted Washington, allowing the Continental Army to score that amazing December 26, 1776 victory.

The Culper spy ring learned that Benedict Arnold was a notorious traitor who was planning on surrendering West Point to the British in 1780. As Arnold's treason was revealed, the Patriots were also able to capture British Major John Andre, who was head of British intelligence. Because Andre was captured in civilian clothes, the Patriots executed him under the "rules of war" at the time, which decimated British intelligence operations.

The Culper spies also learned of a planned ambush on Washington when he went to meet the French high command in 1781. The ambush was foiled and the alliance proceeded.

The ring also foiled at least one assassination attempt on Washington.

With a crew like the Culper Ring watching his back, Washington was free to focus his attention on solidifying the American-French alliance and defeating the British on the battlefield.

QUOTES ABOUT RELIGION

- "Of all the animosities which have existed among mankind, those which are caused by a difference of sentiments in religion appear to be the most inveterate and distressing, and ought most to be deprecated." - Washington in a letter to Sir Edward Newenham of Ireland on October 20, 1792, referencing the enduring conflict between Catholics and Protestants in that country.
- "My fervent supplications to that Almighty Being who rules over the universe; who presides in the councils of nations; and whose providential aid can supply every human defect." - Washington's First Inaugural Address on April 30, 1789.
- "The Hand of Providence has been so conspicuous in all this, that he must be worse than an infidel that lacks faith, and more than wicked, that has not gratitude enough to acknowledge his obligations."
- "Being no bigot myself, I am disposed to indulge the professors of Christianity in the church that road to heaven which to them shall seem the most direct, plainest, easiest and least liable to exception."
- "Religion and morality are the essential pillars of civil society."

CHAPTER 17

WINNING THE WAR, WITH THE FRENCH

Today, the French get a lot of flak throughout the United States and the world; quite possibly, some of it is deserved. After all, the French brought us mimes (what is the deal there?), crepes (just eat a pancake), and a bunch of ugly little cars back in the 1970s. I'm actually joking a little, because when you get down to it, France has given the world a whole lot more.

The modern ideas of democracy and republican government were first articulated by French writers such as Jean-Jacques Rosseau and Voltaire, the concept of the encyclopedia came from France, and the first hot air balloon ride took place in France. These are just a few of the many things that particular country has brought us.

And not only was France a leading cultural and scientific center in the 1700s, but it was also a major military power. Actually, after Britain, France was *the* military power.

So when the American Revolution broke out in 1775, the French were anxiously waiting to see how they could exploit the situation. When they finally did come around to helping the Patriots, it wasn't necessarily because they believed in the cause. Yes, there were some Frenchman, such as the Marquis de LaFayette, who genuinely believed in American independence, but most of the French just saw the conflict as a way to weaken Britain.

And always the pragmatist himself, Washington was more than eager to invite the French into America and accept their help.

Winning the War

After the French joined the cause in 1778, they gave the Americans much-needed funding, materials, and naval support, but they only contributed a limited amount of men on the ground. That was until French General Jean-Baptiste Rochambeau landed in Rhode Island with 6,000 men in 1780. They were met by Washington and the Continental Army in the spring of 1781.

Washington then had to make the biggest decision of his career: attack New York, which was in their grasp, or march south to defeat British General Cornwallis in Virginia?

Washington wanted to take New York. To everyone who knew Washington, it was clear that New York was always on his mind. He took losing it very personally and getting it back was a major reason for the Culper Ring.

Still, Washington was an intelligent man, a pragmatist, and also a diplomat. So he listened to what his other generals and the French had to say.

General Rochambeau wanted to march south to meet the French fleet in the Chesapeake Bay. He argued that this was their true chance to defeat the British for good and that if Cornwallis fell, so too would New York.

Washington listened to Rochambeau and on October 19, 1781, the American and French forces defeated Cornwallis at Yorktown, Virginia, assuring American independence.

So, you see, the French were once pretty badass themselves!

And Washington showed that winning a war and being a true badass is more than just leading troops into battle and killing more of the enemy. Being a true leader involves making wise decisions and probably a lot more give than take. Washington proved that a good general has to be as much of a diplomat as a warrior.

When it came down to it, Washington didn't let his pride get in the way of winning the war.

QUOTES ON DIPLOMACY

- "Observe good faith and justice towards all Nations. Cultivate peace and harmony with all."
- "The nation which indulges towards another an habitual hatred, or an habitual fondness, is in some degree a slave. It is a slave to its animosity or to its affection, either of which is sufficient to lead it astray from its duty and its interest." - Washington's Farewell Address to the nation on September 19, 1796.
- "There never was a law yet made, I conceive, that hit the taste exactly of every man, or every part of the community; of course, if this be a reason for opposition, no law can be executed at all without force, and every man or set of men will in that case cut and carve for themselves; the consequences of which must be deprecated by all classes of men, who are friends to order, and to the peace and happiness of the country."
- "There is nothing so likely to produce peace as to be well prepared to meet an enemy." - Washington in a letter to Elbridge Gerry on January 29, 1780.
- "Be not glad at the misfortune of another, though he may be your enemy."

CHAPTER 18

RETIREMENT ISN'T FOR EVERYONE

When the Treaty of Paris was signed in 1783 ending the American Revolution and officially granting the United States of America independence, Washington returned to Mount Vernon for some much needed R&R. He truly felt at home, and at peace, back where he grew up with those he loved, doing what he loved on the plantation. Although not particularly old, at 51, Washington also wasn't a spring chicken, especially not by 18th-century standards.

So Washington intended to retire to his plantation just like the ancient Roman senator Cincinnatus, against whom he was often compared.

But America was one hot mess after the Revolution.

The "states" in the United States actually refer to the fact that the original 13 states were essentially independent nation-states. Each had its own laws and regulations and wanted to keep it as such. So when the 13 colonies came together during the Revolution, they had to form a sort of unified front, and a type of national government, which was outlined under The Articles of Confederation.

The Articles of Confederation recognized almost no central authority, which meant that New York (the nation's capital at the time) had almost no taxing power, couldn't raise an army, and even had problems with diplomacy. The system left the individual states open to foreign attacks and fostered disunity.

The Founding Fathers knew that a new system needed to put in place to keep the new country together, so James Madison and Alexander Hamilton came up with the United States Constitution.

Well, I'm obviously downplaying it quite a bit to say they "came up" with it, but the idea of the government that still exists today in the United States was first articulated by those men and accepted by each state. The Constitution was set to go into effect in January 1789, but the country needed congressmen, senators, and most importantly, a president.

Hamilton and Madison were well-respected men among their peers and throughout America, but the truth is they were a couple of nerds. That's not to put down to them; they were bright men who gave a lot to the young country, but they weren't the type of men the new country needed to lead it.

The United States of America needed a true badass to guide it through its infancy.

Did Anyone Else Even Run?

You're probably wondering if anyone even ran against Washington in the 1788 presidential election. Well, the answer to that question is a bit complicated, although the easy answer is no.

When it was decided that the United States would have a new constitution, the election of the president became a paramount concern. The president would serve as head of state, commander of the armed forces, and would be a symbol of American power and diplomacy to the world. It was obvious that the presidency was a badass office, so the Founders decided that only a badass of Washington's magnitude could fill it, at least for the first couple of terms.

Although Washington was at first reluctant, he eventually agreed to "run" for president. I say run in quotations marks because no one was even thinking about running against him. Would you?

I also wrote it that way because instead of having months of campaigning before the election, candidates at that time just put their names on a list and waited for everyone to vote for them. It could take a very long time, too, because of the limits of transportation and technology at the time.

But when the votes of the first US presidential election were finally counted, it was no surprise that Washington won about 100% of the vote. The real race was for vice president, which John Adams won. Washington's political victory was as absolute as any of his many military victories. It was so impressive in fact that if he wanted, he could have been made king or emperor.

In fact, there were many in American who wanted to replace George III with George Washington as king of the new nation, but Washington politely declined. As badass as the thought of being king may have been, Washington knew that the new nation needed a different kind of leader.

QUOTES ABOUT GOVERNMENT

- "The spirit of encroachment tends to consolidate the powers of all the departments in one, and thus to create whatever the form of government, a real despotism. A just estimate of that love of power, and proneness to abuse it, which predominates in the human heart is sufficient to satisfy us of the truth of this position." - From Washington's Farewell Address to the nation on September 19, 1796.
- "This contrast between the situation of the people of the United States, and those of Europe is too striking to be passed over, even by the most superficial observer, and may, I believe, be considered as one great cause of leading the people here to reflect more attentively on their own prosperous state, and to examine more minutely, and consequently approve more fully of the government under which they live, than they otherwise would have done." - Washington in a letter to the Marquis de LaFayette on July 18, 1791.
- "Precedents are dangerous things; let the reins of government then be braced and held with a steady hand, and every violation of the Constitution be reprehended: If defective let it be amended, but not suffered to be trampled upon whilst it has an existence." - Washington in a letter to Henry Lee on October 31, 1786.
- "I rejoice that liberty . . . now finds an asylum in the bosom of a regularly organized government; a government,

which, being formed to secure happiness of the French people, corresponds with the ardent wishes of my heart, while it gratifies the pride of every citizen of the United States, by its resemblance to their own." - George Washington on the French Revolution.

- "Liberty, when it degrades into licentiousness, begets confusion, and frequently ends in tyranny or some woeful confusion."

CHAPTER 19

THE FATHER OF A NATION

When Washington was elected, the new nation was on a high and everyone reveled in their new status as Americans, their freedom from Britain, and the fact that they had nearly unanimously elected a total badass to lead them into the future. The country was united, even more so than during the Revolution—in fact, more so than it ever would be.

But almost from the beginning, there were signs of trouble in paradise.

It's important to know that the Founding Fathers weren't monolithic in their political opinions. They all shared the belief that the States should be free from Britain, and that Constitution would provide the best form of government moving forward, but after that, there were some big differences.

And the differences were represented by two men—Alexander Hamilton and Thomas Jefferson.

The Fight against Political Parties

From the beginning, Washington opposed "political factionalism," which he knew could give rise to political parties. The problem was, though, that as soon as he was elected it was clear there were two opposing views of the future of America.

Alexander Hamilton believed that the country needed a stronger central government for protection against foreign powers and to enhance trade. He thought that American industry should be promoted and that it should be protected with tariffs. In foreign affairs, Hamilton believed that the US should re-forge ties with Britain.

Hamilton's beliefs became popular in the Northeast and with merchants. Followers of this philosophy eventually organized into the Federalist Party.

Opposed to Hamilton was Thomas Jefferson. Jefferson believed that America's future was with farmers and ranchers (and slave owners, for that matter). Jefferson was against tariffs, as farmers at that time had to import many of their tools, and he was also against a strong central government.

Jefferson's philosophy was popular in the South and West, and its adherents organized to form the Democratic-Republican Party.

Needless to say, Washington was dead-set against the formation of political parties and really anything that would divide Americans. So, he appointed both Federalists and Democratic-Republicans to key government posts and tried to listen to Hamilton and Jefferson equally.

But no matter what Washington did, the conflict couldn't be stopped, and the US was bound to have political parties. As badass as Washington was, there was probably no badass short of a dictator who could have stopped the formation of political parties in the United States.

Quotes about Political Parties and Politicians

- "However [political parties] may now and then answer popular ends, they are likely in the course of time and things, to become potent engines, by which cunning, ambitious, and unprincipled men will be enabled to subvert the power of the people and to usurp for themselves the reins of government, destroying afterwards the very engines which have lifted them to unjust dominion." - Washington's Farewell Address to the nation on September 17, 1796.
- "The alternate domination of one faction over another, sharpened by the spirit of revenge natural to party dissension, which in different ages and countries has perpetrated the most horrid enormities, is itself a frightful despotism. But this leads at length to a more formal and permanent despotism."
- "I am heartily disposed to entertain the most favourable sentiments of our New Ally, and to cherish them in others, to a reasonable degree, but it is a maxim founded on the universal experience of Mankind, that no Nation is to be trusted farther than it is bound by its interest, And no prudent Statesman or politician will venture to depart from it. In our circumstances, we ought to be particularly cautious for we have not yet attained sufficient vigor and maturity to recover from the shock of any false step, into which we may unwarily fall." - Washington in a letter to Henry Laurens on November 14, 1778.

- "There is an opinion that parties in free countries are useful checks upon the administration of the government, and serve to keep alive the spirit of liberty. This, within certain limits, is probably true, and, in governments of a monarchical cast, patriotism may look with indulgence, if not with favor, upon the spirit of party. But in those of the popular character, in governments purely elective, it is a spirit not to be encouraged."
- "I shall never ask, never refuse, nor ever resign an office."

CHAPTER 20

MODERNIZING AMERICA

As political factions quickly formed, so too did other problems that Washington had to face, foremost of which was how to bring the new country into the modern era. The United States was a rural, agrarian society at the time, much like Europe had been 100 years prior. And as Washington and the United States were struggling to get off the ground, Europe was racing headlong into the Industrial Revolution.

Many in America, including Washington, feared being left behind.

Although Washington wanted to avoid taking sides in the growing battle between Hamilton and Jefferson, he knew that many of Hamilton's ideas were needed to modernize the new country.

The growing political tensions were also sectional and economic in nature. Many of the northern states were in debt after the war and wanted the other states not in debt, or with little debt—most of which were in the South—to help pay their debts. As the Congress was at a seeming impasse over the issue, many looked to Washington for his opinion on the matter, but he decided that discretion was the better part of valor.

The Compromise of 1790

Hamilton worked behind the scenes to come up with a compromise that placed the future capital on the Potomac River, which southern representatives wanted, with debts of the states being forgiven through an aggressive aid package that included tariffs.

If you remember, the Federalists wanted tariffs, so it was their first clear political victory.

And as much as Washington didn't want to appear as if he was favoring one side or the other, Hamilton's plans were too good to put aside. Under Hamilton, who was Washington's Secretary of the Treasury, the First Bank of the United States was established, the United States Mint went into business, and taxes were levied on distilled spirits. Almost immediately, it all seemed to pay off, as the new American economy started kicking.

Foreign powers, including the British, were getting in line to do business with the Americans. Europeans knew that there was a lot of money to be made in America, and at the same time, American entrepreneurs—the type of Americans championed by Hamilton—were doing well.

In fact, it seemed as if almost all Americans were doing well under Washington's presidency and economy. The first rule of modern politics is to keep the people fed, employed, and happy, and there's no doubt that Washington was doing that during his first term.

Well, of course, not everyone was happy...

QUOTES ABOUT ETHICS AND MORALITY

- "Rise early, that by habit it may become familiar, agreeable—healthy—and profitable. It may for a while, be irksome to do this; but that will wear off; and the practise will produce a rich harvest forever thereafter; whether in public, or private Walks of Life." - Washington in a letter to his stepson, George Washington Parke Custis, on January 7, 1798.
- "Labor to keep alive in your breast that little spark of celestial fire, called conscience."
- "I shall not be deprived ... of a comfort in the worst event, if I retain a consciousness of having acted to the best of my judgment." - Washington in a letter to Colonel Basset on June 19, 1775.
- "Happiness and moral duty are inseparably connected."
- "Make it an invariable rule to be in place (unless extraordinary circumstances prevent it) at the usual breakfasting, dining, and tea hours. It is not only disagreeable, but it is also very inconvenient, for servants to be running here, & there, and they know not where, to summon you to them, when their duties, and attendance, on the company who are seated, render it improper." - Washington in a letter to his stepson, George Washington Parke Custis, on January 7, 1798.

CHAPTER 21

WHISKY IS FINE, BUT REBELLION ISN'T

It's hard to say what Washington was feeling when he was serving in his two terms as the Father of the Nation. Although George did leave behind a fair amount of writings, he didn't really get into his "feelings" much. Most men back then didn't think, write, or talk like that either, so unfortunately, we are left to guess.

It's probably safe to say that he was on an emotional high when he first came into office. The country overwhelmingly, almost unanimously, supported him, and it seemed as though there was a general agreement among the leaders about how things were to be run.

But then the conflict between Hamilton and Jefferson took place.

This was a conflict that would become more apparent after Washington left office, but it was already beginning when George was president. From what he said about political parties generally, it's safe to say that he didn't feel very good about the situation.

Still, it seemed as though *the people* would support Washington fully, no matter what.

Well, not all of the people were happy with Hamilton's economic proposals, especially his plan to tax domestically distilled beverages. By that time, whiskey had become Americans' favorite booze and it was a big part of the frontier economy—attempts to regulate or tax it were seen as tyrannical by the distillers.

And the whiskey tax became a sectional and political issue, with the distillers primarily being frontiersman and Democratic-Republicans, while those who supported the tax were from the Northeast and Federalists.

But the tax would go forward and rebellion would ensue. It proved to be the first true test of George Washington's badass credentials during his presidency, which he passed with flying colors.

The Whiskey Rebellion

The excise tax, which quickly became known as the "whiskey tax," quickly set off a series of protests, riots, and assaults on tax collectors throughout the frontier, with western Pennsylvania being the epicenter of the protest movement. And as the protests grew from sporadic outbursts to a full-scale rebellion, Washington was faced with his first test: how to deal with the rebels of what became known as the Whiskey Rebellion?

If he came down too tough on them, he'd look like a hypocrite and a tyrant. He risked not only alienating a large share of the country before his second term but possibly seeing several states break off from the Union.

If he did little or nothing, then he risked sending the message that he had no authority, which would hamper the central government's ability to collect taxes. Worse yet, it would send the message to other nations that the United States was ripe for the picking.

So, Washington decided to wait and let the situation play itself out, although unfortunately for him, things got worse.

The Rebellion finally reached a crescendo in 1794, during the middle of Washington's second term.

On July 16, 1794, an American Revolutionary veteran named James McFarland, who was leading a force of about 600 rebels, was shot and killed by soldiers.

Washington decided it was time for action, so he dusted off his old general's uniform, got on his white horse, and rode at the front of a 13,000 man army to Pittsburgh. Now, that alone is pretty badass for a sitting president to do, but even more badass is that all the rebels went home when they heard Washington was on his way.

They knew that their fight was lost before it even began.

But what's even more badass about the Whiskey Rebellion is how Washington decided to treat the rebels. He could have had them arrested by the hundreds, confiscated their property, and generally ruined their lives as "insurrectionists." Instead, Washington decided to let bygones be bygones.

Washington's choices proved to be the correct ones, as the American republic grew stronger after the Whiskey Rebellion.

QUOTES ON REPUBLICANISM AND DEMOCRACY

- "The very idea of the power and the right of the people to establish government presupposes the duty of every individual to obey the established government." - Washington at his 1796 Farewell Address to the nation.
- "In a free and republican government, you cannot restrain the voice of the multitude."
- "As Mankind becomes more liberal, they will be more apt to allow that all those who conduct themselves as worthy members of the community are equally entitled to the protections of civil government. I hope ever to see America among the foremost nations of justice and liberality."
- "It always has been, and will continue to be, my earnest desire to learn and to comply, as far as is consistent, with the public sentiment; but it is on great occasions only, and after time has been given for cool and deliberate reflection, that the real voice of the people can be known." - Washington in a letter to Edward Carrington, May 1, 1796.
- "Democratical States must always feel before they can see: it is this that makes their Governments slow - but the people will be right at last." - Washington in a letter to Marquis de Lafayette on July 25, 1785.

CHAPTER 22

EVERY BADASS LEADER GETS A MYTH

The Founding Fathers looked to the ancient Romans for inspiration in government, ethics, and philosophy. Rome, when it was a republic, was looked at by the Founders as an ideal form of government and the men who ran it as near as possible as humans can be to perfect rulers. This is how and why Washington acquired the nickname Cincinnatus, after a Roman statesman who could have been a dictator but instead chose to live out his life on his farm.

The Romans also created a myth about the formation of their city and the life of its founder, Romulus. And just like the Romans and Romulus, early Americans also attributed some myths to George Washington. They weren't as cool as Romulus being raised by a wolf, but they are pretty badass nonetheless and chances are you have heard at least a couple of them.

I Cannot Tell a Lie

The most famous myth surrounding George Washington is that when he was about six-years-old he cut down a young cherry tree on the grounds of Mount Vernon. When his father asked if he did the deed, George replied, "I can't tell a lie, Pa; you know I can't tell a lie. I did cut it with my hatchet."

George's dad then embraced him for telling the truth instead of punishing him for the vandalism.

The truth is, though, the story is totally contrived.

So how did this myth enter the American consciousness?

Well, it was first circulated in print in the early 1800s by historian Parson Weems. Weems was as much of a Washington fanboy as he was a historian, so whenever he had a chance to play up the positive qualities of the Father of the Country, he did. Gradually, as something like that gets repeated enough, people begin to believe it. It didn't hurt that many artists offered their own interpretations of the event in paints, the most notable being Grant Wood's 1939, *Parson Weems' Fable*. As the title indicates, Woods made no attempt to promote the historicity of the event and even depicted young Washington with an adult head, which is more than a bit creepy, if you ask me.

Still, most people tend to believe that the event took place, which is probably as much of a testament to the enduring perception of Washington as an honest person as it is to the lack of critical thinking skills of the general population.

Another enduring, although not so glamorous myth about George Washington was that he had false teeth made of wood. Yes, Washington had lost most of his teeth by the time he became president, and he did in fact wear dentures, but technology at the time was advanced enough that the dentures were made from ivory or human teeth.

Other myths surrounding Washington include that he requested Betsy Ross to sew the first American flag. Ross was a flag maker during the War, but there's no evidence the two met.

Then there is the White House.

During Washington's presidency the US capital was in New York and Philadelphia. The city of Washington was still a dream, and the first president had no direct involvement in the planning of it or the White House.

It's true that some of these myths are a little silly and not really important in the historical sense, but if anything, they reinforce what a badass Washington really was. I mean, how many other presidents - or world leaders of any country or time period, for that matter - have so many myths floating around about them?

George Washington certainly has to be at or near the top of that list.

Inspirational Quotes by Washington

- "Let your heart feel for the afflictions and distress of everyone, and let your hand give in proportion to your purse."
- "One of the difficulties in bringing about change in an organization is that you must do so through the persons who have been most successful in that organization, no matter how faulty the system or the organization is."
- "It is better to offer no excuse than a bad one." - Washington in a letter to his niece Harriet Washington on October 30, 1791.
- "Citizens by birth or choice, of a common country, that country has a right to concentrate your affections. The name of AMERICAN, which belongs to you, in your national capacity, must always exalt the just pride of Patriotism, more than any appellation derived from local discriminations." - Washington's 1796 Farewell Address to the nation.
- "I cannot conceive a rank more honorable, than that which flows from the uncorrupted choice of a brave and free people, the purest source and original fountain of all power." - Washington in a letter to General Thomas Gage after he was informed that he was made the commander of the Continental Army.

CHAPTER 23

NO QUESTIONS OF FRAUD IN THAT ELECTION

Several of the last few American presidential elections have been close, with accusations of voter fraud and interference being flung from both sides. It's all really a sign of how divided the United States is today and how far it has come since the days of Washington.

Washington was elected president with almost unanimous support and his re-election in 1792 wasn't much different.

Despite the whiskey tax and the growing tensions between the Hamiltonians and Jeffersonians; Washington was able to keep both men working together in his cabinet, and most importantly, he was able to keep the country united.

The way in which the president and vice president were elected was also a little different back then. Yes, the electoral college elected the president through representatives of each state as it does today, but voting was a ranked-choice style: The person with the most votes became president, while number two was vice president. This changed with the Twelfth Amendment in 1804 to the system we have today, but in 1792, it made things a little more interesting.

Perhaps the most badass aspect of the 1792 election was that Washington didn't campaign and didn't even indicate much of a desire for a second term. Still, the Federalists and Democratic-Republicans urged him to run again. Well, he didn't really run because he never really campaigned. So, I guess you could say he threw his hat in the ring for a second term.

The true race was for vice president, which again went to John Adams.

Of the states that chose their electors by popular vote at the time (all states do so by a popular vote today), nearly all went 100% for Washington. The only state that didn't was Pennsylvania, where a lot of people were still bitter about the Whiskey Rebellion. Even so, Washington still won over 75% of the vote in the Keystone State.

Overall, it was another impressive electoral showing for the first president, but things were rapidly changing in the country and the world.

In Washington's second term, he would truly have to show plenty of people that he was still a badass and that despite being a young nation, America was not to be messed with.

Quotes on Politics, Politicians, and Policy

- "The common and continual mischiefs of the spirit of party are sufficient to make it the interest and duty of a wise people to discourage and restrain it." - Washington's 1796 Farewell Address to the nation.
- "There is an indissoluble union between a magnanimous policy and the solid rewards of public prosperity and felicity."
- "In vain would that man claim the tribute of Patriotism who should labour to subvert those pillars of human happiness, these firmest props of the duties of Men and Citizens. The mere Politician, equally with the pious man, ought to respect and to cherish them." - Washington's 1796 Farewell Address to the nation.
- "The foundation of our national policy will be laid in the pure and immutable principle of private morality."
- "My observation is that whenever one person is found adequate to the discharge of a duty ... it is worse executed by two persons, and scarcely done at all if three or more are employed therein."

CHAPTER 24

WASHINGTON AND THE WORLD

So we've seen that although George was given the nearly unanimous support of the American people, he still had a number of issues to deal with during his presidency. Things weren't always easy and he learned that was especially true in the realm of foreign affairs.

Washington found that he couldn't just sit there and be the pleasant plantation owner from Virginia when he was dealing with some pretty pressing issues of the time. Washington and the American people would quickly learn that although the US was separated by oceans and wilderness from most other countries, the world was becoming a lot more connected in the late 1700s, so what happened to one nation would affect others.

Washington soon realized that when it came to foreign affairs, the more things changed, the more they stayed the same.

Same Old - Same Old

After Washington was elected president, war broke out again between the French and British. It's not really important how or why it happened, other than they were the two biggest boys on the block at the time. The American people were still firmly pro-French, but Hamilton and his faction were pro-British, so once more Washington was caught in the middle. In the end, Washington declared neutrality, which wasn't seen favorably by the French, who believed that the Americans should join their side as their allies in thanks for French help in the American Revolution.

On the other hand, the British had no respect for American neutrality, confiscating American ships and imprisoning American sailors, and keeping forts on the American frontier. British agents played a major role in instigating the American Indian Western Confederacy to go to war against the United States in the Northwest Indian War (1785-1795) as well.

To add to all this, French authority totally collapsed in 1789 during the French Revolution, which ended up being a dark version of the American Revolution: The clergy and nobles were targeted and executed, and the country descended into an orgy of violence that only ended with the rise of Napoleon.

Then there was the revolution in Saint-Domingue (the island that contains the modern countries of Haiti and the Dominican Republic).

Both revolutions caused political problems for Washington, as he came to power through a revolution but opposed both of those revolutions due to their high levels of violence directed towards civilians.

In the end, Washington avoided renewed conflict with the British, or with any other nation for that matter. But he did send troops to fight an enemy overseas, sort of.

Quotes on Foreign Affairs

- "My policy has been, and will continue to be, while I have the honor to remain in the administration of the government, to be upon friendly terms with, but independent of, all the nations of the earth. To share in the broils of none. To fulfil our own engagements. To supply the wants, and be carriers for them all: Being thoroughly convinced that it is our policy and interest to do so." - Washington in a letter to Gouverneur Morris in 1795.
- The duty of holding a Neutral conduct may be inferred, without any thing more, from the obligation which justice and humanity impose on every nation, in cases in which it is free to act, to maintain inviolate the relations of Peace and amity toward other Nations.
- "Against the insidious wiles of foreign influence . . . the jealousy of a free people ought to be constantly awake."
- "History and experience prove that foreign influence is one of the most baneful foes of republican government."
- "But if we are to be told by a foreign Power . . . what we shall do, and what we shall not do, we have Independence yet to seek, and have contended hitherto for very little."

CHAPTER 25

WASHINGTON PROTECTS THE WAVES

In the previous chapter, I mentioned how American ships and sailors were routinely captured by the British. The only thing the Americans could do about it was to build a navy. That may seem like an easy decision to make, but at the time, many in Congress believed it was a waste of money that would only anger the European powers.

Still, Jefferson pushed the idea of a navy and Washington agreed.

The reason for creating a navy was primarily due to pirates; not in the Caribbean, as most people think, but in the Mediterranean. You see, at the time, piracy was a big thing on the North African or Berber coast, which was known at the time as the "Barbary Coast." Muslim pirates from the Barbary Coast, with the blessing of various Berber and Ottoman rulers, would capture European ships for supplies and slaves. By the late 1700s, most European nations had developed navies powerful enough to repel the pirates, but without the protection of the British Navy, the Americans were easy prey.

So, the idea to build a navy became a pressing concern in Washington's second term. The president got together with the leaders of the two major factions in Congress, and they came up with the Naval Act of 1794, which opened the way for the construction of frigates.

So, how did the Act immediately affect the situation? Actually, very little. The pirate attacks on American ships continued and both the British and French navy's continued to impound American ships and sailors.

But that situation wouldn't continue for long.

The government quickly built a small but effective navy, so that by the early 1800s, the Americans were able to resist British impressment and put an end to the Barbary Pirates attacks.

QUOTES ABOUT THE MILITARY

- "To be prepared for war is one of the most effectual means of preserving peace." – Washington's address to Congress on January 8, 1790.
- "While I repeat my obligations to the Army in general, I should do injustice to my own feelings not to acknowledge in this place the peculiar Services and distinguished merits of the Gentlemen who have been attached to my person during the War. It was impossible the choice of confidential Officers to compose my family should have been more fortunate. Permit me Sir, to recommend in particular those, who have continued in Service to the present moment, as worthy of the favorable notice and patronage of Congress." – Washington's resignation of his command of the Continental Army on December 23, 1783.
- "To expect ... the same service from raw and undisciplined recruits, as from veteran soldiers, is to expect what never did and perhaps never will happen. Men, who are familiarized to danger, meet it without shrinking; whereas troops unused to service often apprehend danger where no danger is."
- "Soap is another article in great demand--the Continental allowance is too small, and dear, as every necessary of life is now got, a soldier's pay will not enable him to purchase, by which means his consequent dirtiness adds not a little to the disease of the Army." – Washington in a letter to the Continental Congress on July 19, 1777.

- “Military arrangement, and movements in consequence, like the mechanism of a clock, will be imperfect and disordered by the want of a part.”

CHAPTER 26

KEEPING UP APPEARANCES

George Washington may have been America's first badass-in-chief, but even he wasn't bad enough to stop health ailments from slowing him down. Although the 18th century was the Age of the Enlightenment, with great advances being made in medical science, most treatments still lagged far behind what we know today—or what was known even 100 years later, for that matter.

Due to illnesses taking many of his family members at relatively young ages, George was a bit of a fitness nut for his era, watching what he ate, drinking alcohol only in moderation, and even exercising. Still, it wasn't enough to keep Washington from catching smallpox, losing most of his teeth, and contracting a number of other health ailments, several of which become quite severe during his presidency.

But like a true badass, Washington never let on to outsiders that he was ill.

Washington had to have a tumor removed on June 17, 1789, that was so bad that it prevented him from walking or sitting properly. It also took six weeks for the wound to heal.

As bad as the tumor was, it was nothing compared to what George faced in the spring of 1790.

Late winter and early spring are often prime seasons for influenza, which was rampant around Philadelphia in 1790. The president caught the illness. Then, as if catching the flu in the 1700s wouldn't have been bad enough, to make matters worse, it progressed to pneumonia.

Things looked pretty grim for Washington. His hearing and sight were starting to go and became so bad that Massachusetts Congressman Theodore Sedgwick stated that on May 16 the attending doctors "had no hopes of his recovery."

Yet just when all seemed lost, Washington showed everyone what a badass he was by not only pulling through but also by returning to work within a few days. Sometime later, Washington wrote about his battles with illness:

> *Within the last twelve months I have undergone more, and severer sickness than thirty preceding years afflicted me with, put it altogether—I have abundant reason however to be thankful that I am so well recovered.*

Washington would continue to battle health problems for the remainder of his life, and eventually, succumb to them, but the true victory he achieved was keeping up appearances. George knew that it was imperative to project an image of strength and stability for the new nation, no matter how weak or ill he may have felt at the time. So, by continuing to conduct business as usual, he was able to give the country the fighting chance it needed to make it through the first few tough years.

Quotes on God, Religion, and Spirituality

- "May the father of all mercies scatter light, and not darkness, upon our paths, and make us in all our several vocations useful here, and in His own due time and way everlastingly happy." - Washington in a letter to the Hebrew Congregation of Newport, Rhode Island on August 17, 1790.
- "Now therefore I do recommend and assign Thursday the 26th day of November next to be devoted by the People of these States to the service of that great and glorious Being, who is the beneficent Author of all the good that was, that is, or that will be - That we may then all unite in rendering unto him our sincere and humble thanks - for his kind care and protection of the People of this Country previous to their becoming a Nation." - Washington's proclamation of the first Thanksgiving on October 3, 1789.
- "I beg you be persuaded that no one would be more zealous than myself to establish effectual barriers against the horrors of spiritual tyranny, and every species of religious persecution."
- "May the children of the stock of Abraham who dwell in this land continue to merit and enjoy the good will of the other inhabitants-while every one shall sit in safety under his own vine and fig tree and there shall be none to make him afraid. May the father of all mercies scatter light, and

not darkness, upon our paths, and make us all in our several vocations useful here, and in His own due time and way everlastingly happy."

- "You, Gentlemen, act the part of pious Christians and good citizens by your prayers and exertions to preserve that harmony and good will towards men which must be the basis of every political establishment; and I readily join with you that "*while* just government protects all in their religious rights, true religion affords to government its surest support." - Washington to the Synod of the Dutch Reformed Church in North America on 19 November 1789.

CHAPTER 27

GOODBYE AMERICA

Today, the US president is limited by two terms in office under the Twenty-Second Amendment to the United States Constitution, which became law in 1951. The amendment was passed not long after President Roosevelt died during his fourth term in office; despite him being an extremely popular president, most believed that four terms were simply too long in office.

Most also believed that three terms were too long in office, so both parties agree that the limit should be two terms.

Before Roosevelt, however, the reality is that most presidents, even very popular ones, only served two terms anyway. With that said, there still wasn't a law that said presidents couldn't run for a third or fourth term. Since Washington was so revered throughout American history, there was basically an unwritten rule, mostly followed, that since Washington only served two terms, other presidents should not serve longer than that.

There was also the age and health issue. Most men aren't young when they become president, so after eight years of constant stress, the vast majority were ready to go home. And not long after being re-elected, Washington too was ready to go home.

This isn't to say that he "phoned it in" during his second term. We've seen how Washington was quite active, effective, and badass during his second term. But we also saw how he battled health problems. By 1796, he was well into his sixties, which was pretty old by 1700s standards. Washington could have easily won a third term, but he had done what he needed to do. George had managed to win a war, become the father of a nation, and overcome illnesses, so it was time for him to return home to spend his final years in rest and contemplation with his family.

But before he left, he had one last thing to do.

Washington's Farewell Address

Washington's second term was hectic, to say the least. In addition to facing the British, Indians, the French Revolution, pirates, political parties, and all the other assorted growing pains of a new nation, Washington had to think about the future. Ever the selfless man, when Washington thought about the future, it wasn't *his* future necessarily, but that of all his countrymen.

So, not long after being re-elected, when he wasn't dealing with all of the issues discussed earlier, he sat down to write his "Farewell Address" to the nation. Farewell addresses are now standard issue for American presidents leaving office, but as it was a new thing at the time, Washington knew that it had to be perfect.

Washington's address was also different from those today because it wasn't delivered to a crowd. Instead, it was published in writing for the public to read.

Another attribute of badasses throughout history is that they know their limitations and how to work around those potential barriers. Washington, while being a great leader of men on the battlefield and in the halls of government, was never an accomplished academic like many of his fellow Founding Fathers. He was very conscious of this, so when it came time to draft the Farewell Address, he asked for assistance from his fellow Virginian and architect of the Constitution, James Madison.

After Madison wrote the initial draft, Washington read it and sent it to Alexander Hamilton for more advice.

Washington no doubt did this to promote a sense of unity in the government, which was one of the central tenants of his Farwell Address: Madison the stalwart Democratic-Republican and Hamilton the Federalist, cooperating to articulate Washington's vision of a future America.

In the end, Washington's address was one of a positive future, written in a style that was plain and to the point like Washington, yet flowing with a style that belied its ghostwriters.

Despite its positive tone, Washington warned against things that in retrospect seem eerily prescient. He pointed to sectionalism as a threat to the union's stability; with the potential to not only stifle the development of the new country, but also to bring it down. He stated that political parties were to be avoided because they placed narrow loyalties above country and pitted Americans against each other. Finally, although Washington advised against isolationism, he also warned against becoming too involved in the affairs of other countries, which could eventually lead to heavy foreign influence in America.

To just about anyone who reads Washington's farewell address, it's obvious how badass his perceptions about the world really were.

Many people also ask themselves, "What would things be like if we'd have listened to Washington?"

Quotes on Economics and Business

- "The North, in an unrestrained intercourse with the South, protected by the equal laws of a common government, finds, in the productions of the latter, great additional resources of maritime and commercial enterprise and precious materials of manufacturing industry. The South, in the same intercourse, benefiting by the agency of the North, sees its agriculture grow and its commerce expand. Turning partly into its own channels the seamen of the North, it finds its particular navigation invigorated; and, while it contributes, in different ways, to nourish and increase the general mass of the national navigation, it looks forward to the protection of a maritime strength, to which itself is unequally adapted." - From Washington's 1796 Farewell Address.
- "It is incumbent upon every person of every description to contribute to his country's welfare."
- "In the present State of America, our welfare and prosperity depend upon the cultivation of our lands and turning the produce of them to the best advantage."
- "No taxes can be devised, which are not more or less inconvenient and unpleasant; that the intrinsic embarrassment, inseparable from the selection of the proper objects (which is always a choice of difficulties), ought to be a decisive motive for a candid construction of

the conduct of the government in making it, and for a spirit of acquiescence in the measures for obtaining revenue, which the public exigencies may at any time dictate." – From Washington's Farewell Address.

- "The West derives from the East supplies requisite to its growth and comfort, and, what is perhaps of still greater consequence, it must of necessity owe the secure enjoyment of indispensable outlets for its own productions to the weight, influence, and the future maritime strength of the Atlantic side of the Union, directed by an indissoluble community of interest as one nation." – From Washington's Farewell Address.

CHAPTER 28
ENJOYING RETIREMENT

When Washington's second term was up, he knew that he couldn't carry out the duties of office with the vigor required, so he decided to leave the country in the hands of someone else. So, Washington left Philadelphia with honor and retired to Mount Vernon.

Washington began his retirement on March 9, 1799, with a six-day trip from Philadelphia to Mount Vernon. Once back in Virginia, Washington wanted to do nothing other than restoring his dilapidated plantation and spend time with his wife and grandchildren. He worked with his slaves and day laborers, rising every day at about 5 a.m. to rebuild the buildings on the plantation that had fallen into disrepair and to construct new ones.

Not bad for a 65-year-old with chronic health conditions!

George seemed to find a new sense of purpose in this late phase of his life; all those who knew him at this time saw him as being happy and at peace.

But Washington was a consummate warrior, and there was still at least one more battle to be fought in his life.

Politics Never End

Although Washington warned of the evils of political parties in his farewell address, the problem was already present and wasn't going anywhere. The second president was John Adams, who openly identified as a Federalist. Adams defeated Thomas Jefferson, who was a vocal Democratic-Republican, in the 1796 presidential election, ensuring that partisan politics would become a mainstay of the American system. And as much as Washington never wanted partisan politics to happen, there was nothing he could do to stop it.

And partisan politics even threatened to ruin Washington's retirement.

As much as Washington wanted to stay out of the growing battle between the Federalists and Democratic-Republicans (often just abbreviated to "Republicans" by 1800), he felt compelled to offer his assistance for the good of the country. Washington did so with completely honest intentions, but he was often met with resistance and sometimes chicanery from members of both parties.

Leading Republicans began to publicly attack some of Washington's policies, which just a couple of years before would have been unthinkable. But you know what they say: A year is a lifetime in politics.

When George visited Washington in 1799 just before the opening of the White House, he decided to unleash a torrent of criticism on the French Revolution, which was fully supported by the Republicans.

In the end, Washington felt a bit dejected by the political situation, but it didn't keep him from his activities at Mount Vernon. He continued to work there every day, riding his horse for several hours at a time to make sure the business was running properly. Truly a physical badass until the end, Washington died at age 67 of an inflammation of the throat on December 14, 1799, at his home and surrounded by family.

It's perhaps a bit ironic that something as seemingly innocuous as a sore throat killed such a badass, but that's the way things happen sometimes. Even badasses die and how and when they go, especially in the 1700s, is often the result of chance.

QUOTES ABOUT FATE, HUMAN NATURE, AND DESTINY

- "Can it be, that Providence has not connected the permanent felicity of a Nation with its virtue? The experiment, at least, is recommended by every sentiment which ennobles human Nature. Alas! is it rendered impossible by its vices?" - From Washington's 1797 Farewell Address.
- "There is a Destiny which has the control of our actions, not to be resisted by the strongest efforts of Human Nature." - Washington in a letter to Mrs. George Willian Fairfax on September 12, 1758.
- "Next Monday the Convention in Virginia will assemble; we have still good hopes of its adoption here: though by no great plurality of votes. South Carolina has probably decided favourably before this time. The plot thickens fast. A few short weeks will determine the political fate of America for the present generation, and probably produce no small influence on the happiness of society through a long succession of ages to come." - Washington in a letter to Marquis de Lafayette, May 28, 1788.
- "We must take human nature as we find it. Perfection falls not to the share of mortals. Many are of opinion that Congress have too frequently made use of the suppliant humble tone of requisition, in applications to the States, when they had a right to assume their imperial dignity

and command obedience." - Washington in a letter to John Jay on August 15, 1786.

- "You may believe me my dear Patsy, when I assure you, in the most solemn manner, that, so far from seeking this appointment I have used every endeavor in my power to avoid it, not only from my unwillingness to part with you and the Family, but from a consciousness of its being a trust too great for my Capacity and that I should enjoy more real happiness and felicity in one month with you, at home, than I have the most distant prospect of reaping abroad, if my stay were to be Seven times Seven years. But, as it has been a kind of destiny that has thrown me upon this Service, shall hope that my undertaking of it, is designed to answer some good purpose." - Washington in a letter to his wife on June 18, 1775.

CHAPTER 29

FREEING HIS SLAVES AS THE LAST ACT

In the United States' current political climate, just like so many things today, George Washington's views on race and slavery have become quite divisive. On one side, there are those who focus on the fact that Washington was a slave owner and did nothing to really promote racial egalitarianism, or even abolition, for that matter.

On the other side are those who prefer to see the more positive attributes of George Washington. They argue that slavery was an ingrained institution of the period and that any views Washington had on race or slavery that may seem offensive today need to be understood in the context of the time.

As with most things, though, the truth concerning Washington's views on race and slavery can be found somewhere in the middle.

The Peculiar Institution

Slavery was an ingrained part of George Washington's life. He knew it from the time he was born, as his family owned plenty of slaves, and it continued to play an important role until his death. Slaves worked the plantation at Mount Vernon and helped Washington to expand it, and when Washington married, he inherited even more slaves from his wife.

But Washington's true views on racial issues are actually a bit more complex than this situation might suggest.

Although it's true that Washington profited from slavery for his entire life, he also went out of his way to keep slave families together, generally avoided the use of corporal punishment, and most importantly, left a provision in his will that all slaves at Mount Vernon were to be freed upon Martha Washington's death.

Martha freed all the Mount Vernon slaves one year after George's death.

Washington was also close to one of his slaves, William Lee, who became his personal attendant and, at times, a confidant. Lee rode with Washington into battles on numerous occasions and served him during his time as president. Lee was also the only slave Washington freed outright in his will.

Many historians have written that Washington's views on slavery changed after the Revolution. He began to see the hypocrisy of the institution in the new nation and hoped that it would eventually be eliminated. Though Washington's views on slavery were tempered by the Revolution, however, they became somewhat harsher toward American Indians.

Washington viewed the numerous Indian tribes as sovereign nations and acquired a great amount of respect for them when he served in the French and Indian War. But when

Washington became president, the Americans were already involved in a protracted war against several tribes in the Northwest Indian War.

Washington made it a top priority to defeat the Western Indian Confederacy in the war and clear the Northwest (now Ohio and Indiana) for American expansion and settlements. If the American Indians were going to be a part of Washington's vision for America, he reasoned, they would have to become farmers.

This was a paternalistic attitude, with Washington believing that the Indian tribes must be "taught" the intricacies of Western Civilization, such as writing, Christianity, and democracy - whether they wanted to or not.

The truth is, though, no matter what views Washington may have had on slavery, the Indian question, or race in general, they were always his own and he never ran from them. True, he was influenced by the time in which he lived, but he also displayed an incredible amount of independent thought on these most controversial subjects. Washington made his way through life adjusting his beliefs according to his own observations and experiences.

Washington may not have always thought the way some today would have liked him to think, but he was always true to himself and as authentic as anyone can get, and that alone is pretty badass.

QUOTES ON SLAVERY, RACE, AND ETHNICITY

- "I am glad you have brought three of the Children of your principal Chiefs to be educated with us. I am sure Congress will open the Arms of love to them, and will look upon them, and will look upon them as their own Children, and will have them educated accordingly. This is a great mark of your confidence and of your desire to preserve friendship between the Two Nations to the end of time, and to become One People with your Brethren of the United States. My ears hear with pleasure the other matters you mention. Congress will be glad to hear them too. You do well to wish to learn our arts and ways of life, and above all, the religion of Jesus Christ." – Washington to the chiefs of the Delaware Indians, who had sent three of their boys to be educated in Philadelphia on May 12, 1779.

- "I can only say that there is not a man living who wishes more sincerely than I do to see a plan adopted for the abolition of slavery."

- "Upon the decease [of] my wife, it is my Will and desire th[at] all the Slaves which I hold in [my] own right, shall receive their free[dom] . . . . The Negroes thus bound, are (by their Masters or Mistresses) to be taught to read and write; and to be brought up to some useful occupation, agreeably to the Laws of the Commonwealth of Virginia, providing for the support of Orphan and other poor

Children. And I do hereby expressly forbid the Sale, or transportation out of the said Commonwealth, of any Slave I may die possessed of, under any pretence whatsoever." - From George Washington's will.

- "I had always hoped that this land might become a safe & agreeable Asylum to the virtuous & persecuted part of mankind, to whatever nation they might belong; but I shall be the more particularly happy, if this Country can be, by any means, useful to the Patriots of Holland, with whose situation I am peculiarly touched, and of whose public virtue I entertain a great opinion." - Washington in a letter to Francis Adrian van der Kemp on May 28, 1788.
- "The policy or advantage of [immigration] taking place in a body (I mean the settling of them in a body) may be much questioned; for, by so doing, they retain the language, habits, and principles (good or bad) which they bring with them. Whereas by an intermixture with our people, they, or their descendants, get assimilated to our customs, measures, and laws: in a word, soon become one people."

CHAPTER 30

SO BADASS THAT COUNTLESS MONUMENTS, MONEY, AND TOWNS ARE NAMED AFTER HIM

So now that we've taken a stroll through the amazing life of the First President, it's easy to see why he was such a badass. But just like all true badasses, Washington continued to inspire awe and impress people long after he died. In fact, he still does today, as shown by his place at the top of most list of the Americans' best or most popular presidents.

Because of Washington's generally badass nature, he adorns the name of places and things all over the United States, and his image has been worn into the minds of not just Americans, but people all over the world.

It's pretty incredible when you think about it.

The fact that George Washington died decades before photography was even invented hasn't stopped people from knowing his image whenever they see it. The average American likely recognizes Washington's image just as much, if not more, than most of the recent American presidents.

There's no doubt that Washington's presence loomed large over the United States and has continued to do so in the more than 200 years since his death.

And it isn't hard to see Washington's influence all across the United States.

Washington Is America and America Is Washington

If one way to gauge a level of a person's badassness is the number of monuments and other places named after them, then there's no doubt that George Washington is #1 in the USA. The number of memorials and monuments are too many to go into here, so let's just take a look at the most important ones.

Many presidents have memorials, statues, and monuments of them located throughout the country, but the three most notable ones in Washington, D.C. are dedicated to Washington, Jefferson, and Lincoln.

The Washington Monument, which is a 555-foot-tall Egyptian style obelisk, was built from 1848 to 1884 and designed by Robert Mills. Standing as a towering guardian over the capital city, the Washington Monument is truly a testament to Washington's strength and love of the city.

And while we're talking about legacies and DC, how much more badass can you get than to have the capital city of your nation named after you!?

The other world famous monument of Washington is the sculpture of his likeness—along with those of presidents Lincoln, Jefferson, and Teddy Roosevelt - in South Dakota.

The masterpiece was designed by sculptor Gutzon Borglum and was finished in 1941. It depicts Washington's face, located in front of the others, looking pensively out into America.

It's definitely a pretty badass accomplishment that two of the greatest monuments in the nation are dedicated to Washington's life, but the list of memorials and dedications just keeps going and going and going…

In 1932, Washington's image began appearing on the quarter coin, which was in addition to his likeness already on the $1 bill. You may be surprised - or not - that Martha Washington also appeared on $1 bills in the 1800s.

Then there are the numerous "Washingtons" you can visit throughout the country. Actually, there's so many that you'll have to try to *avoid* going through a place called Washington in the United States!

Washington is the only president to have a state named after him. There are also 31 counties, more than 241 townships, and dozens of cities and towns named after the first president.

Countless elementary schools, colleges, and vocational schools are also named for Washington. Washington's name has also been given to dozens of parks, smaller monuments, streets, and neighborhoods, from sea to shining sea. It doesn't matter the region of the US you're in, or the state, for that matter - you're sure to drive through, near, or stop at a place named for Washington.

There's no doubt that Washington continues to permeate every aspect of American culture and will continue to do so for the foreseeable future. Truly, there's no American president that says "American" more than George Washington himself, and that's pretty badass!

Quotes on Happiness

- "I have too much of the vanity of human affairs to expect felicity from the splendid scenes of public life. I am still determined to be cheerful and to be happy in whatever situation I may be, for I have also learnt from experience that the greater part of our happiness or misary depends upon our dispositions, and not upon our circumstances; we carry the seeds of the one, or the other about with us, in our minds, wherever we go." – Martha Washington in a letter about George's career in public service to Mercy Otis Warren on December 26, 1789.
- "Republicanism is not the phantom of a deluded imagination. On the contrary, laws, under no form of government, are better supported, liberty and property better secured, or happiness more effectually dispensed to mankind."
- "Interwoven is the love of liberty with every ligament of the heart."
- "The United States enjoy a scene of prosperity and tranquility under the new government that could hardly have been hoped for."
- "I very linearly [sic] wish you would exert yourself so as to keep all your matters in order your self without depending on others as that is the only way to be happy to have all your business in your own hands." – Martha Washington.

CONCLUSION

Among all types of people, there is what is known as a "prototype"—the first of their kind, the one who establishes how all those who follow are measured and compared. There are several different badass prototypes throughout world history, but when it comes to American history, and especially American presidents, there can be only one: George Washington.

In many ways, George Washington epitomized what it means to be a badass in the United States, as he talked the talk and walked the walk every day of his life. From successful plantation owner and businessman to war hero, revolutionary, and eventually the Father of the Country, there's no doubt that George Washington was an epic badass who influenced the course of history not just in America, but throughout the world.

But we must recognize that Washington had his fair share of setbacks and hardships on the road to badass stardom.

George lost loved ones, suffered some major defeats on the battlefield, and witnessed the rise of partisan politics under his presidency. Yet all of those setbacks proved to be stepping stones for greater victories and leaps forward—Washington never stayed down for long and always learned from his defeats, which is perhaps what separated him from other men of the time.

Washington may not have been the most intelligent of the Founding Fathers, but he definitely was the most effective. And effectiveness is what the Patriots needed in their darkest hours.

Sure, the intellectual ideas and guidance that Madison, Hamilton, and Jefferson gave the Patriot cause was invaluable, but when it came down to it, the Patriots needed a tough, plain-talking tough guy who could sock the British in the mouth on the battlefield.

In other words, the Patriots needed a true badass more than anything if they hoped to win their independence. George Washington proved to be exactly that man.

And when the country needed a badass again, to lead them through the first few awkward years of uncertainty, Washington answered the call. Washington may not have wanted to be the president, and he certainly didn't revel in the limelight in the way many presidents have, but he made it his duty to lead the country to the best of his ability through an unprecedented political era.

There's no doubt that, when John Adams gained the presidency, due to Washington, the country was in a stable, safe, and prosperous state.

Finally, if you don't think all of that is enough to prove how badass George Washington was, you only need to look around the country at all the monuments, memorials, parks, towns, and counties named after him. Only a true badass could garner that much reverence and respect, which is why the First President consistently ranks as the top president.

It's true that Washington was complex and seemingly contradictory to the average modern person. He was a revolutionary who believed in using force against those who rebelled against his government if necessary. He came from wealth and privilege, but was often more comfortable working next to people of lower socioeconomic classes than going to dinner parties among the upper crust. Washington was a slave owner, but he also emancipated his slaves and favored the gradual abolition of slavery in the United States.

Yes, George Washington may have been mythical in some ways, yet he was still human.

For all of these reasons, George Washington is not only the greatest badass president but also probably the greatest badass American in history.

DON'T FORGET YOUR FREE BOOKS

GET THEM FOR FREE ON
WWW.TRIVIABILL.COM

MORE BOOKS BY BILL O'NEILL

I hope you enjoyed this book and learned something new.

Please feel free to check out some of my previous books on Amazon.

Made in the USA
Monee, IL
02 January 2022